Plainville Turkey Farm
1923 - 2007

by Robert W. Bitz

LCCN: 2012920629
ISBN-13: 978-0-9859504-3-9
First edition, published 2012.

Ward Bitz Publishing
Baldwinsville, NY

The author may be contacted at:
P.O. Box 302
Plainville, NY 13137

Front cover picture: Plainville's version of Norman Rockwell's painting Freedom from Want.
Robert and Janice Bitz are presenting a Plainville roast turkey to some of Plainville's team members.

PREFACE

The commercial turkey industry was in its infancy when Plainville Turkey Farm came into existence in 1923. Turkey meat was a delicacy, not affordable for most Americans, and only available for the Thanksgiving and Christmas holidays. Although turkeys had been domesticated for well over 1,000 years, they still resembled their wild cousins that were designed to survive in the wild, and able to fly to the tops of trees and run like a deer.

Native Americans, in Central America, had domesticated the turkey. Turkeys were taken to Europe on one of Columbus's ships and then transported back across the Atlantic with settlers coming to New England, over 100 years later. Here, it was crossed with the wild turkeys of New England and changed little, even after all of its travels to Europe and back to America.

In 1923, although incubators had been in use for some time, the majority of turkeys were still hatched under mother hen turkeys or under chicken hens that served as surrogate mothers. Thousands of farmers kept a few turkeys for breeding and grew a flock of 20 to 100 using this method. Only 25 years earlier, drovers still gathered a few turkeys from each of a number of farmers as they drove the turkeys to markets in large cities. Trucks with internal combustion engines, paved roads and incubators, combined to open the pathways toward commercial turkey production.

Plainville Turkey Farm had its beginnings as these three factors came together. Plainville was different in two ways, however. It hired people who owned incubators to hatch the turkey eggs it produced and it sold all of its turkeys after they had been bled and their feathers removed. It also continued a variation of the practice by drovers, dating back for more than 100 years. Rather than driving the turkeys to market, Plainville took trucks loaded with crates to farms, some distance from markets and bought their small flocks of turkeys. These turkeys were transported back to Plainville, fattened and then dressed and sold in the Syracuse area. This practice continued for over a decade, until the late 1930s.

Because refrigeration was almost nonexistent in the early days of the turkey industry, and because man hadn't learned to trick turkeys into laying eggs except in the early spring were two powerful reasons why turkey was only available at Thanksgiving and Christmas. Marketing turkeys in NY dressed form (bled and with just feathers removed) coupled with the colder days of November and December solved the problem of lack of refrigeration, and subjecting turkey breeders to artificial light fooled the turkeys into thinking it was spring any time of the year. Thus artificial light and refrigeration made it possible for turkeys and turkey products to be available for the consumer all times of the year.

Although disease prevention, nutrition practices and marketing were still in their infancy, during the 20s and 30s, it was an opportune time to start in the turkey business. With good management and marketing skills, growing turkeys was profitable. But, even more important, the consumption of turkey meat was beginning to increase. Although per capita consumption was less than four pounds in the 40s, it gradually increased to 20 pounds, 50 years later, during a period when the United States population more than doubled. Additionally, by producing dressed birds with brand identification Plainville was able to gradually build a loyal clientele. From Plainville's very beginning it attached a readily visible red tag to each dressed turkey's leg, identifying the turkey as being a Plainville turkey. This identification and a continuous emphasis on quality paid dividends.

There were several other factors that helped Plainville prosper. It practiced early vertical integration. Manure from the turkeys helped produce good crops of corn, wheat and oats that were fed to the turkeys. It started manufacturing its own feed rather early, for a farm, eliminating the middle man and helping ensure high quality feed. It not only processed its turkeys but did much of its own marketing, including retail sales directly to the consumer. It was also one of the first to recognize potential opportunity in turkey further processing and the development of products that would be used by customers 52 weeks of the year.

As one reads this book it becomes very obvious that I am proud of what my family and hundreds of our fine team members accomplished over 85 years. Plainville Turkey Farm started as one of many thousands of farms, in this country, that grew a few turkeys. Gradually Plainville Turkey Farm increased in size and by the 1980s produced most of the turkeys grown in NY State. They were some of the finest turkeys ever produced: turkeys fine, not only in taste, but also nutritionally. The turkeys were also grown in an animal friendly environment, which undoubtedly improved their quality. Even though we marketed over a million turkeys, each of the last few years we owned Plainville Turkey Farm, we were a small operation compared to most of the competition from other parts of the country.

Grandfather, Dad and even myself had no clue as to what Plainville Turkey Farm might become but always attempted to do the best we could. My son Mark had a vision of what Plainville might become and pointed it in the direction where our turkeys and turkey products could fill a niche that large companies ignored. It was the right choice at the right time.

TABLE OF CONTENTS

ONE

1923 to 1939

Turkeys came to Plainville through a stroke of fate. Dad and Grandfather regularly sold their potatoes at the Syracuse Public Farmer's market. In November 1923, a small turkey grower from Northern New York had eight live turkeys that he had been unable to sell at the market, the market was closing, and he did not want to take them home. My dad bought them and brought them to our farm at Plainville to fatten them up and take back to the market, along with his potatoes, for sale at Christmas time.

Apparently Dad and Grandfather enjoyed the turkeys because the next year a small flock of turkeys became part of the farm's operation. After a few years several thousand were being grown and our farm became one of the earliest commercial turkey operations. My dad and grandfather, however, never regarded turkeys to be more than just a part of their farm operation since they never increased production beyond a few thousand turkeys. They continued to have a dairy herd and grow a variety of crops including cabbage, potatoes, beans, peas, corn, wheat, oats, hay, and tobacco.

Arthur Hudson, a friend and former neighbor, soon joined them in a three-way partnership. Grandfather died in 1934 and a successful partnership between my dad and Arthur continued until 1939, when Arthur and four of his sons started their own farming operation.

It took very little equipment to start growing a few turkeys. A former chicken house was large enough to brood 300 turkeys. It was on the edge of an apple orchard that could be fenced and offer shade and pasture for the turkeys. The farm was already growing corn, oats and wheat, which could be used for most of the feed needed for the turkeys. Some farm lumber was used to make a few feed troughs and some empty barrels were cut in two to furnish tubs to hold water for the turkeys. Probably less than 100 turkeys were grown the first year.

One end of the tobacco shed with an opening to an outside pasture area was used for turkey breeders. Eggs were saved from late February through June and taken to a hatchery every two weeks where the poults were picked up four weeks later. About 1945, the turkey breeder flock was discontinued and poults were purchased from a hatchery twice a year; in early April for the Thanksgiving market and the middle of June for the Christmas market.

As turkey production increased, sun porches were built that fitted against the south side of each small brooder house to provide extra space and to harden the turkeys before they were moved to pasture. Simple range shelters on large runners were also built to provide protection from both sun and rain. Because of the runners a team of horses could easily move the range shelters to keep fresh pasture available for the turkeys.

Because of owls, foxes and even human predators, a man stayed with the turkeys at night, especially when they were nearly grown. He had a small building with a stove and bed, along with a dog tied outside the building to alert him of any intruders. He also had a loaded shotgun, ready to use. In the 30s and early 40s, live turkeys in a field were a temptation to some people, and although

A picture from a 1933 article in the Syracuse Post Standard *of Robert Bitz and Olin Hudson taking the first step toward preparing a Plainville turkey for some customer's Christmas dinner.*

we never caught anyone, we saw evidence of their visits.

Dad learned from his experience the previous year that it was more profitable to sell turkeys that had been killed, and with their feathers removed. The stripping room in the old tobacco shed was an ideal spot for that part of the operation. There was a stove with an open water tank on top that had been used to provide high humidity in the room, when stripping tobacco, and that served as a tank for scalding the turkeys. They quickly learned that the traditional method of pulling the dry feathers (dry picking) from the turkeys was extremely labor intensive. As a result, killing the turkeys by bleeding, scalding them in hot water to easily remove the feathers and then putting the turkey in a brown paper grocery bag was all that was needed to prepare the turkeys for market.

No refrigeration was needed to keep the turkeys cold, partially because it was cool at Thanksgiving and Christmas time and because there were no openings cut in the turkey for bacteria to enter. Poultry prepared in this manner was referred to as New York dressed even though it might have occurred in California or Massachusetts. New York dressed was the common method used throughout the world at that time. The internal organs were removed by the consumer at home or in the butcher shop just before the customer received the turkey.

My parents never told me much about their turkey operation during its first decade. I have a copy of a Syracuse newspaper showing Olin Hudson and myself pretending to cut off the head of a turkey in 1933 when we were three years old. The article indicates that several thousand turkeys were being grown then.

It is likely that the size of the turkey crop had been increased by 200 or 300 turkeys each year during the previous decade. Caring for the turkeys would not have taken much additional labor. Since Dad had a hired man and Arthur had several boys, and with a few neighbors to help prepare the turkeys, marketing could be accomplished in a three day pre holiday window before any turkeys had time to spoil.

As mentioned earlier, the first turkeys came from a farmer who had grown them in Northern New York. Dad and Arthur continued to buy turkeys from Northern New York farmers at holiday time.

A 1930s picture of the sign at Plainville Turkey Farm promoting their milk fed turkeys. The barn on the left is where the dairy cows were kept. However, the milk from the cows was sold, and skim milk was purchased from area creameries, for two and one- half cents a gallon, to feed the turkeys.

Two trucks were loaded with empty crates and traveled north, in the middle of the night, to arrive at daylight before farmers' turkeys went wandering off in the fields. The turkeys were unloaded at our farm and fed for a few days before being slaughtered. There were quite a few farmers that grew 25 to 50 turkeys and had no way to market them who were pleased to sell the turkeys.

The process of slaughtering and removing the feathers was quite simple as long as you understood what was necessary to prepare a desirable product. A light rope was put around the turkey's legs and it was hung from a long pole set in the ground at a 20 degree angle so the turkey's head was about waist height. A narrow knife was inserted in the turkey's mouth to cut the arteries and not leave any visible external cuts. Next the turkey was carried into the stripping room where its legs were dry picked. It was then scalded at 210 degrees and the rest of the feathers removed. After the feathers were removed the turkeys were put in a large open top stock tank of cold water to cool. About 15 minutes later the turkey was hung from a tobacco hanger to dry and was soon ready to be put in a bag for delivery to a store.

Gradually minor improvements were made. Parchment bags were put around the dressed turkey's head and a red tag, aout the size of a dollar, was tied to one of the dressed turkey's legs. The red tag was printed with the farm's name and the words, "If satisfied tell others, if not tell us." It also carried the words, "Fancy Milk Fed Turkeys." There was also a large sign next to the road with the words, "Plainville Turkey Farm," "Fancy Milk Fed Turkeys."

There were several creameries and cheese factories within 20 miles of the farm that had little use for their skim milk and sold it quite cheaply. Dad loaded several empty barrels on the truck, three times a week, and went to the creamery to buy skim milk. Morning and evening, when we fed the turkeys, we poured some of the skim milk on their mash. The turkeys loved the milk and it provided them with some needed nutrients.

A circa 1935 picture of a turkey breeder flock at Plainville Turkey Farm. The turkeys could go in and out of the barn on the right, which had originally been a tobacco shed. Notice the roosts on the left, which were a substitute for trees where wild turkeys enjoyed roosting. The center area of the tobacco shed with the windows was where the turkeys were processed.

3

A flock of bronze and White Holland turkeys on range in the 1930s. The small building on the right is where a man slept at night with his dog and loaded shotgun nearby. In the background is a tall pole with a fox trap on top to catch Mr. Owl when he flew down to look over the flock before he selected his turkey dinner.

A flock of turkeys being fattened for Christmas dinners. Most of them are bronze but there is a Narragansett turkey in the foreground. The turkeys could go in and out of the tobacco shed on the left.

When we started removing the head, feet and intestines, it was another step toward meeting the customer's needs. Most of the stores still bought our turkeys New York dressed and performed that task at the store. It was not uncommon for a store-keeper to buy live turkeys, not from us but from other farmers, and do the slaughtering in the basement or behind the store. I remember a store in Auburn performing this task into the 1960s.

In 1939, when Dad and Arthur amiably ended the partnership, they divided the customers between them and each one continued to grow and market their own turkeys. After a few years, Arthur decided to discontinue growing turkeys and instead went into chicken egg production. Dad continued growing turkeys and the next chapter describes some things that happened between 1939 and 1950.

A 1930s picture of Harry Bitz in a flock of turkeys, about 18 week old, between his house and Gates Road. The farm's hog pen is the building in the rear and the orchard of apple and pear trees is on its right.

A 1937 photo of Bob Bitz, Gates Hudson and Arthur Hudson moving NY dressed turkeys, with horses and bobs, from the tobacco shed to hang in the cellar of the house overnight, to keep the turkeys from freezing. Bob, like most boys, is making the most of the process by putting his foot on the back of the runner and riding along.

A 1936 turkey growers' educational program sponsored by Ralston Purina Co. at the Plainville Turkey Farm. Harry Bitz is explaining to the visitors how turkeys are dressed for marketing and his partner Arthur Hudson is standing in the doorway.

1939 to 1950

Arthur Hudson and Dad had grown 6,000 turkeys as a partnership in 1938, and each one grew 3,000 the next year. They each took one-half of the range shelters, brooder houses, fence materials and feeders so there was little that either one had to buy. By dividing the customers between them, each one could continue in business and not be concerned about a market.

Most of Dad's 3,000 turkeys were dressed for sale on the Saturday, Sunday, Monday and Tuesday before Thanksgiving and during a similar time period before Christmas. Each day we dressed between 300 and 400 turkeys. We went to the turkey pasture with a wagon, loaded with crates to catch the turkeys, the afternoon of the day before they were to be slaughtered. A fenced pen had been set up that gradually narrowed to only three feet in width, yet was large enough to hold 200 turkeys. About 20 turkeys were driven at a time into a wire sided box with a trap door that slid down to trap the turkeys. Part of the top of the box opened so a man could reach into it to catch each turkey by its legs. The turkey was passed to a man on the wagon who put the turkeys into crates. When the wagon was loaded we transported the crates to the barn and set them near where they would be killed the next day.

Each year some hens and a few toms were kept for breeders. The toms were put with the hens during the latter part of February and the eggs from the hens were saved for hatching during March, April and May. Eggs were taken to a turkey hatchery near Watertown every two weeks and the

poults were picked up four weeks later. The first few eggs laid, before they were saved for hatching, my mother used for cooking. Even when we were saving the eggs for hatching there were occasional cracked, soft-shelled or double yolked eggs that were used for cooking. If there were more eggs than we needed for eating, I sold them on the market and was able to keep the money.

Dad rented a farm with a large barn two miles from where we lived. The turkey breeders were kept in its basement. Each evening, during the breeding season, we removed any hens, called setters, that were in the nests. These hens had decided it was time to quit laying eggs. They thought they were ready to start a family but we had other ideas. We put them in a special pen, for a few days, without roosts and an uncomfortable wire floor to try to break them of their family ideas.

Prior to collecting eggs, each hen and tom was tattooed with a specific number marked on one of its wing webs. A blood sample was taken from each turkey and sent to a laboratory to be tested for pullorum, a salmonella bacterial disease. If a turkey tested positive, it had to be located and destroyed. Fortunately we never had a reactor and didn't have to search through the flock to find one.

Another unusual aspect of turkey breeding was putting a saddle on each hen turkey. Natural mating was used and during the act of mating the sharp toes on the toms tore the backs of the hens. To prevent this, a heavy cotton saddle, covering her back, was attached to both of the hen's wings to provide protection. I would hazard a guess that very

A circa 1950 aerial view of Plainville Turkey Farm. The garage with a freezer inside, built in 1949, is next to the two houses. The turkey processing building is the other building with a new metal roof and was built in 1950. The tobacco shed, where turkeys had been processed before 1950, is to the right of the new processing plant. Notice two brooder houses with turkeys on each sunporch in the lower right.

few of my readers ever realized that turkeys had a form of protected sex!

The eggs, now fertile because of the introduction of toms to the pen with the hens, were gathered daily, cleaned and placed carefully, pointed ends down, in special boxes, each holding about 200 eggs. The boxes of eggs were placed at a 45 degree angle and turned end to end twice a day to replicate the mother hen turning eggs with her feet in her nest. When the eggs were placed in the incubator, they were turned automatically every four hours.

About 1940, Dad started taking the turkey eggs to Hiscock Hatchery in Skaneateles, which was much closer to the farm. Mr. Hiscock did custom work, hatching chicken, turkey and duck eggs. In 1945, labor shortages during World War II and the ready availability of day old poults brought the end of turkey breeders on our farm. We started buying day-old poults, delivered to our farm, from

Six week old White Holland and bronze turkeys on a sunporch. About two weeks later they were moved to a fenced in pasture.

Bob Bitz and his dog Trixie are ready to feed and water turkeys on a turkey range. On the trailer, by Bob's knee, are 100 pound bags of Beacon feed for the turkeys.

both Timmerman's and Ryor's Turkey Farms near Watertown. This change decreased labor, not only in keeping breeders, but also permitted us to start two flocks a year, one for Thanksgiving and one for Christmas, rather than starting smaller flocks every two weeks and mixing different ages of turkeys in two flocks.

Other advantages of having all the turkeys in a flock the same age were that the feed was designed for each specific age and the turkeys were of a more uniform size at marketing time. Previously we had to sort the turkeys before we processed them to have sufficiently mature birds for processing.

A circa 1950 photo of Dick Doback, a schoolboy from Plainville, filling a feed trough with feed. The wheelbarrow carried the feed to each one of about a dozen brooder houses, and the troughs were filled by hand.

Our methods for growing the turkeys changed very little before the 1950s. The poults were started in small brooder houses holding about 225 each. They were given access to a wire enclosed sun porch at two weeks to provide them with more room and harden them for the move to pasture at eight weeks. Manufactured feed in mash form and in 100 pound bags was purchased from the Beacon Milling Co. at Cayuga. This was supplemented with wheat, oats and corn, also in 100 pound bags, that we had grown on the farm or purchased from other farmers. All of this feed required lifting by hand several times before it was dumped into wooden feed troughs for the turkeys.

We made a two wheel trailer from the rear portion of an old truck and mounted a water tank on the trailer to haul water to the turkeys. Ends, about 12 inches long, were sawed from wooden barrels and were filled with water for the turkeys to drink. Bags of feed were also loaded on the trailer each morning and evening when we went to the fields to feed and water the turkeys.

Turkey nutrition was still in its infancy so we supplemented the feed with skim milk. Two or three times a week our farm truck, with first wooden barrels and later a tank on it, went to a creamery to buy skim milk. Old records show that it cost two and one-half cents a gallon in 1944. A pail of skim milk was poured on top of the mash in the wooden troughs and the turkeys loved it. The minute we started doing this they all hurried in to make sure they got their full share. We advertised our turkeys as "milk fed" and I believe it did improve the growth of the turkey and the flavor of its meat.

A circa 1945 photo of a catching cage being used to catch turkeys for processing.

A circa 1945 photo of live turkeys being transported to the tobacco stripping room for processing. Ralph Vaughn is driving the farm's first tractor, a Farmall F-20. On the wagon from left to right are Harry Bitz, Bob Bitz and Winthrop Van Camp.

From the very beginning of the turkey industry, it had been difficult to grow turkeys. They were subject to disease and predators, which had kept most turkey flocks from being larger than 100 turkeys. In the 1940s, they still possessed most of the characteristics of wild turkeys by being easily spooked, and when frightened would all pile into the nearest corner of a building, smothering the ones underneath. Because of these factors we were fortunate if we were able to market 75% of the ones we started.

World War II brought many changes to our farm. Several of the changes were caused by the shortage of labor, others by government regulation and some because of the increased demand for meat. Numerous items were rationed during the War and one of them was meat. Poultry wasn't rationed but because red meat was rationed there was increased demand for poultry. To help control inflation, the United States established the Office of Price Administration (OPA) and maximum prices were established at both the retail and wholesale level for live turkeys, New York dressed turkeys and turkeys dressed ready for the oven. We discovered that the maximum price set for ready

to cook turkeys was decidedly more favorable than for either live or New York dressed turkeys.. This brought the end of New York dressed turkeys on our farm. Preparing oven ready turkeys created more work but paid very well.

Our farm had no refrigeration to cool the dressed turkeys so we marketed our turkeys within a day of when they were killed. This was especially important if there was a warm spell at Thanksgiving or Christmas. Sometimes at Christmas it was cold enough that any turkeys not marketed the day they were killed would freeze during the night unless we transported them to the cellar in our house. I marvel that we never heard of any spoilage problems even though our methods of dressing and handling the turkeys remained extremely primitive until 1950.

A few more words regarding our primitive turkey dressing facilities, which were very similar to the dressing facilities on other farms at that time. The turkeys were killed across the driveway from where retail customers came to buy our turkeys. As turkeys that were being slaughtered died, the violent flapping of wings threw blood over a wide area. Often a customer had to wait to pass, until the

A group of school children visiting the farm in 1948. Almost all of the children had been given feathers to take home with them. Note the Guernsey cows in the barnyard behind the children.

11

turkeys had quieted down to avoid being splattered with blood. There was no running water in the stripping room where the turkeys were prepared for market. If there was any contamination on a turkey it was wiped off with a much used portion of a feed bag. Unquestionably changes needed to be made!

During World War II Dad was still growing about 3,000 turkeys and could have sold several times that number. We found it necessary to put a sign by the road telling potential customers that we had no extra turkeys for sale. Turkeys were so scarce that Dad hired a night watchman to stay in the stripping room each night after we had dressed turkeys. We also limited each store to the number that they had purchased the previous year. Numerous times Dad was offered money under the table, but he refused to deal in the "black market."

We also reserved the same number of turkeys for sale on the Central New York Regional Market as we had sold in previous years. We had no way of knowing each individual who had previously purchased a turkey so it was 'first come, first serve'. As soon as the market opened at 6:00 a.m. we were mobbed with customers. The market authorities tried to form the customers into a line so there was

Harry Bitz, in 1950, holding two New York dressed toms that weighed a total of 69 pounds.

Picking the feathers from turkeys in 1950. The turkeys were bled and then dipped in 200° water to loosen the feathers, which were then pulled by hand. From left to right are Peg Middlemore Pickard, Tom McGovern, Willard Horle and Nellie Green.

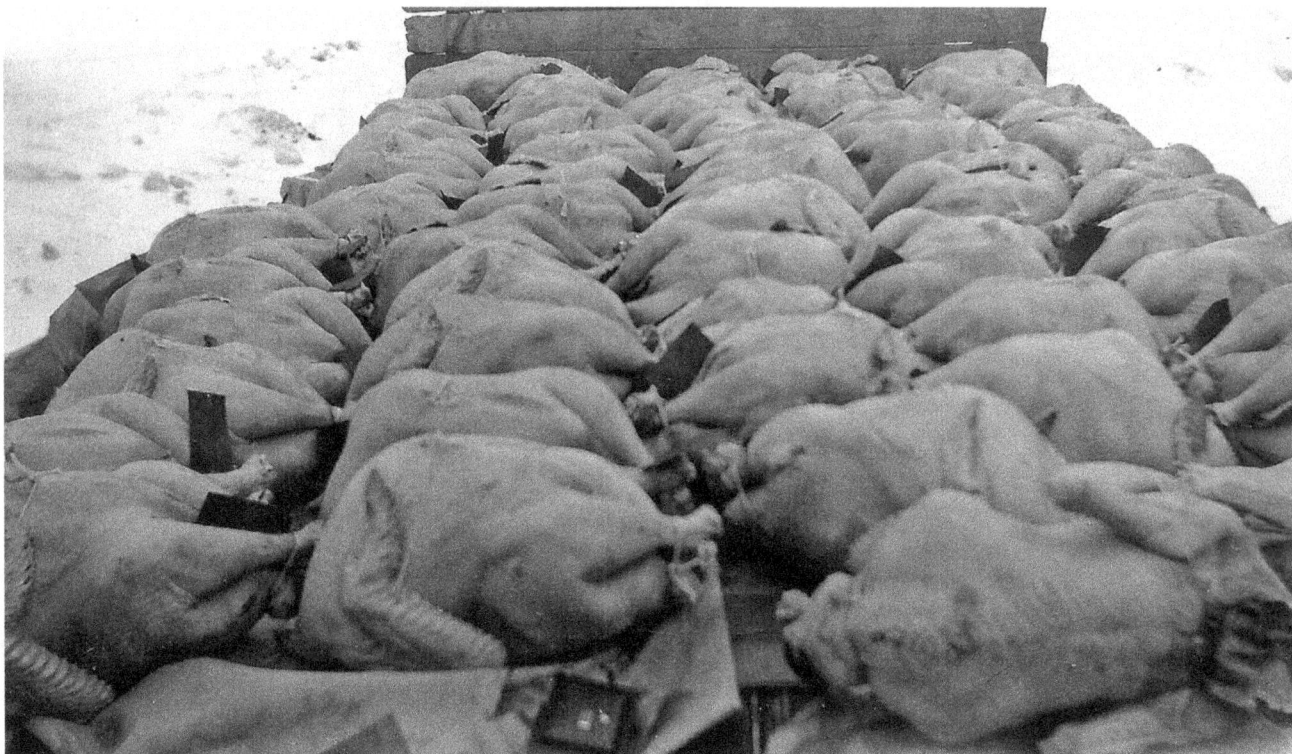

A circa 1948 photo of Plainville turkeys ready for the oven. Notice that there is a large red tag on each turkey, which said "Fancy Milk Fed Turkeys," and also, "If Satisfied Tell Others if Not Tell Us." Each turkey was placed in a large heavy white paper bag before it left the farm.

some semblance of order. We limited the turkeys to one per customer and didn't even need to take them out of their paper bags for customers to see. Normally customers wanted a specific size but during those years they took whatever they could get. The turkeys were sold as fast as we could take the customers' money, about 300 in an hour, whereas it normally would have taken about six hours to sell them.

In 1949, Dad received a letter from the New York State Department of Agriculture and Markets advising him to make substantial improvements to his processing facilities or they would shut him down. The letter came as a shock. However, there was no question that the facilities were totally inadequate. The dressed turkeys were hung on nails protruding from old tobacco hangers. The barn where they were hanging was open to the rafters. Sparrows were flying around above the turkeys and, well, we know what sparrows sometimes do! A ceiling was installed over the dressed turkeys to keep the sparrows away and sufficient other minor changes were made to get approval. We had a good

record without previous complaints, which was in our favor.

The improvements bought us some time but the writing was on the wall. Dad had to decide whether to continue growing and processing turkeys. Continuing would require substantial expense. I enjoyed turkeys and was planning to stay on the farm. This was the deciding factor when we upgraded our processing facility in 1950.

In 1949, while I was in college, due to my encouragement, a four-car garage was constructed with a walk-in freezer in one end that held several hundred turkeys. After Christmas and New Year's Day there was little market for turkeys and the freezer permitted us to dress turkeys that were left over without having to feed and care for them during nasty winter weather. It also allowed us to have turkeys for customers between January and October. From the time we discontinued keeping breeders we had no live turkeys large enough to sell during half of the year. In 1950, we invested in a small dressing plant but that will be part of the next chapter.

A circa 1948 photo of Glenn Bratt and Harold Meaker with a truckload of turkeys for sale on the Central NY Regional Market. Three large tobacco boxes were turned on their side and a sheet of brown tobacco paper was put on top to form a sales table.

The garage constructed in 1949 showing the farm's two trucks and two family cars. The trucks were used for turkey deliveries and the cars were also used to deliver turkeys to retail customers before Thanksgiving and Christmas.

STATE OF NEW YORK
DEPARTMENT OF AGRICULTURE AND MARKETS
C. CHESTER DU MOND, COMMISSIONER
ALBANY 1

BUREAU OF FOOD CONTROL
C. R. PLUMB, DIRECTOR
CHARLES H. FOGG, ASST. DIRECTOR

November 23, 1949

Mr. Harry C. Bitz
Plainville Road
Plainville, New York

Dear Sir:

    We are in receipt of a report of inspection and investigation of your activities in slaughtering and dressing turkeys both for retail and wholesale purposes.

    The building equipment and methods used in this operation are very unsatisfactory to say the least. As a bona fide farmer raising your own domestic turkeys on your own farm you are not subject to the licensing provisions of Article 5 A. However, you are required under Article 5 A and Article 17 to maintain your place of operation in a sanitary condition and perform such operation in a sanitary manner.

    We are taking this opportunity to inform you that the slaughtering and dressing of turkeys for resale must be discontinued at once, and we are notifying our representative to make a reinspection and if you are still operating under these unsatisfactory conditions you will be referred to our Legal Bureau for penalty action.

Very truly yours,

Director

CWN/ms

This is a 1949 letter from the NYS Department of Agriculture and Markets to Harry Bitz advising him that dressing turkeys in the farm's existing facilities must be discontinued immediately. They had been dressed in the same manner for the 26 previous years without any complaints.

Plainville, New York
December 7, 1949

Mr. C. R. Plumb, Director
Bureau of Food Control
Department of Agriculture and Markets
Albany 1, New York

Dear Mr. Plumb:

Your letter of November 23rd came as a complete surprise
to me. IHhave been in the turkey raising business for a
good many years and have built up a reputation for putting
out a high quality type of full dressed bird to trade in the
Syracuse section and over the Regional Market at Syracuse.

Will you please advise me specifically what changes it is
desired that I make. I have received no inspection report
and have been to the Farm Bureau and to the Regional Market
and they are not able to advise me what requirements, if any,
have been set up for grower killing and dressing.

I certainly want every condition satisfactory and sanitary
and I believed that I was accomplishing this.

I do feel that the last paragraph in your letter was rather
harsh.

Very truly yours,

HARRY BITZ

HB:r

*Harry Bitz's reply to NYS Ag and Markets. Unquestionably things needed to be improved and were
improved immediately but nothing had ever been said before. The handwriting was on the wall and a
new processing facility was build the next year.*

1950 to 1966

1950 was a milestone in the development of Plainville Turkey Farm. Although a freezer had been constructed in one end of a new garage the previous year, the new building for processing turkeys gave indications that turkeys would continue to be part of the farm's operation in the future. The new building was modest. It was about the size of a large ranch house with unfinished concrete block walls both inside and outside. It did have drains in its concrete floor, although when completed, it appeared that the contractor thought water ran uphill. For a few years we wore out brooms, sweeping water uphill! There was no refrigeration the first year and the same primitive methods were used to prepare the turkeys for market. It was, however, a move in the right direction.

During the next few years we gradually made improvements that included adding a walk-in cooler with a meat rail system to move turkeys in and out. Wooden tables covered with oilcloth were used for evisceration of the turkeys, the heads were still cut off on a wooden block with a hatchet but there was now running water. About 3,500 turkeys were grown and processed.

In January 1952, I graduated from Cornell (although the official ceremony was in the following June) with plans to go back to the farm and grow turkeys. I had no grandiose plans but hoped to have a successful turkey business. In retrospect, my thinking was small. Having always lived on a small farm and with farms of a similar size throughout the community, I had no idea of the agricultural revolution that was about to take place and what part I might play.

Coincidentally, the day I packed up to leave Alpha Zeta Fraternity, where I was a member while at Cornell, Dad was delivering 150 large New York dressed turkeys to Knight's Public Market in Ithaca. Knight's Market supplied meat to many of the fraternities and sororities at Cornell as well as to the restaurants in the area. When there were large tom turkeys remaining after the holidays, Knight's was a potential customer but at a low price. I drove my car to Knight's Market and helped unload the turkeys. Thoughts were going through my mind concerning how I might avoid having to market surplus turkeys for less than they cost to grow.

Back on the farm I joined Dad and his two hired men, helping with the cows, crops and turkeys. I wanted to move out of all of the enterprises except turkeys but had great respect for my dad and wanted his approval for any changes. I moved slowly and he was most cooperative so we never had conflict. My family was conservative with money, and the only time they borrowed money was from Dad's small insurance policy to help buy turkey feed. With moving forward on a cash only basis, change had to come at a slow steady rate.

Upon my return to the farm, Dad bought a neighboring farm to help increase the size of our business. This farm had been a magnificent farm with a large tobacco operation 70 years earlier but had fallen into a state of disrepair with buildings falling down and weeds thriving. We spent over a year cleaning up the farm. We tore down three

This is an 1878 lithograph of the William Wilson tobacco farm on Plainville Road. Mr. Wilson grew tobacco, bought and sold tobacco and made cigars on the farm.

A 1952 photo of remaining tobacco barns on the William Wilson farm when it was purchased by Harry Bitz to become part of the Plainville Turkey Farm. The large barn on the left was converted into a grain storage building and the barn on the right was converted into a large corn crib.

A horse barn on the William Wilson farm, on the right, was torn down by Harry Bitz in 1952 and the cow barn on the left was remodeled. The basement of the barn was used for turkeys and the upper part was used as storage for hay and straw. The roof, in the middle, extending above the two barns was on a square silo and one of the earliest silos in Central New York.

The barns remaining on the William Wilson farm one year after Mr. Bitz purchased it. A new wall was constructed under the barn on the left and the barn was jacked up two feet to permit gravity loading of bulk grain from the newly installed grain bins on the third floor.

barns and half of the house. A building that had been used as a tobacco warehouse was converted to a granary holding 200 tons, increasing our grain storage seven fold. It was a big deal for me at the time but in retrospect was insignificant compared to the many thousands of tons of storage we had in later years. We designed this granary so we could load a truck for feeding turkeys by gravity. The feeding truck had bins that flowed into bushel containers used to fill the turkey feeders. It was a great improvement over handling 100 pound bags of grain and eliminated the use of bags.

When we repaired the remaining barns on the farm our intent was to keep turkey breeders and buy an incubator. After much consideration we decided it would be wiser to put our emphasis on growing and marketing, while leaving the breeding to others. In retrospect this was one of the wisest decisions we ever made. Sometimes a decision

not to do something is more valuable than the alternative.

All of our day old turkey poults were started in small brooder houses, each with its separate kerosene stove and holding about 200 poults. It was labor intensive and I felt it would be wise to have one large building to start our turkeys. In 1954, after much planning, we constructed an 8,000 square foot pole barn for brooding. It was before pressure treated poles were available so we arranged to have a farmer cut us some small locust trees, which were resistant to rot. We peeled the bark from the trees, dug holes to set them in and constructed the building during the winter and spring with only the assistance of a local carpenter and his helper. Using locally sawed rough lumber and pouring a concrete floor we completed the building in June at a cost of $1.25 a square foot.

Harry Bitz holding a day old poult in the new brooder house. The stoves were heated with propane and the poults were watered and fed by hand the first two weeks. We believed the turkeys needed roosts (later it became obvious they didn't) and dropped roosts down from the ceiling when the poults were two weeks old.

A pole barn with turkeys about 1962. Each metal feeder held about 900 pounds of feed and was filled about once a week from a trailer, with an elevated auger, as a tractor pulled the trailer through the building. Automatic waterers were along both sides of the building.

We started 2,500 poults in early June and a few days later quite a few started to die. We had no idea why they were dying and called in experts from Beacon Milling Company, where we were buying our turkey feed, and from Cornell but no one was able to find the cause. We had a new 'state of the art' building with automatic feeders and waterers and anticipated that the poults livability would be much better. Instead we lost about 40% compared to the normal 10% in the brooder house. Not being able to determine the cause of the mortality, I arranged to purchase 1,500 poults to grow in August to prove whether our trouble had been a one-time occurrence or something else. We needed to use the building successfully the following year or we would be in serious trouble. The August flock did even worse! We lost half of the poults during the first two weeks and quite a few of the remaining ones did not grow well.

However, we found the problem. We had used a deep well to grow turkeys successfully the previous five years. The well had been slightly salty from the beginning but not enough to bother either the turkeys or ourselves. By coincidence the well's salinity had increased at the time we constructed the new brooding building and it was poisoning our turkey poults. In retrospect, it was something that should have been obvious to us. We obtained water from a different well for the next flock and their livability was very good.

Upon returning to the farm, I explored ways to improve our turkey marketing to bring greater profits to the farm. Now that we had a freezer, we began promoting frozen turkeys as gifts from employers in their employees. We used attractive boxes for our turkeys and included a leaflet of cooking instructions along with some attractive shredded cellophane. In 1954, in cooperation with

21

In the late 50s we started driving turkeys to the processing plant rather than catching them and putting them in crates. Our first refrigerated delivery truck is in the background.

Onondaga County Cooperative Extension and the Syracuse Manufacturers' Association, we hosted a turkey barbecue at the farm. This helped make our farm visible to potential buyers of turkeys for Christmas gifts.

There were about 100 New York turkey growers that were members of the New York State Turkey Growers' Association. Each year, at their annual meeting in January they held a dressed turkey contest with prizes for the winners. I entered some of our turkeys in these shows and later in the National Turkey Growers' Association shows. Participation in these shows was to obtain publicity to bring the Plainville Turkey Farm name in front of consumers.

Each year I attempted to increase our turkey production about 10% and in 1959 we produced 12,000. Another larger freezer had been added to our processing plant and I was slowly developing sales, although small, during each month of the year. We still had turkeys on pasture in November, December and January when weather was often not good for the turkeys. In 1956, we constructed an 8,000 square foot pole barn that cost less than $1

a square foot, using inexpensive materials and our regular farm labor. (That building is still strong and sturdy today.) Every year or two, after 1956, we constructed another pole barn in an attempt to have all our remaining turkeys under cover by December. Until 1978, we built all of the pole barns with our own labor to minimize costs.

During this period of time we started poults in only April and June leaving the brooding building

Cynthia Bitz Bowen by a new pole barn being constructed in 1960. One of the old small brooder houses is on the right.

This is the first large turkey growing building on the farm, constructed in 1954. Behind the corn on the left is a concrete ramp used by a tractor to push manure into a manure spreader when cleaning the building. The higher portion of the building housed an overhead feed bin that kept the automatic feeder supplied with feed for the turkeys in the building.

empty from October through March. It bothered me to see the building set idle several months each year so I decided to grow turkey broilers and market them when they weighed five to nine pounds, ready for the oven. I felt this was a size that many families could use conveniently in February or March. When we marketed these turkeys we put them in used wooden meat boxes and packed them in ice. At this time there were almost no further processed turkey products or turkey parts available and we were able to sell them to a chain of independent stores. Acceptance was reasonably good but we were unable to obtain an appropriate profit and discontinued growing turkey broilers.

Upon the construction of a pole barn we decided to go completely to bulk feed and eliminate handling feed in bags. We bought large self feeders, each holding about 900 pounds, and filled them once a week with a tractor powered feed wagon that elevated the feed into the feeders. Instead of feeding the turkeys, cafeteria style, with oats, corn and supplement in separate feeders, we ground and mixed the ingredients together to provide one complete feed. To accomplish this we bought a mix-mill, which metered the correct amount of each ingredient through a hammer mill. The feed was elevated from the mix-mill to one of four overhead steel bins, each of which held feed for turkeys of a specific age.

As we grew more turkeys, removing the feathers required excessive labor. Mechanical pickers had been on the market since the late 40s and we needed to control our labor costs wherever practical. We had purchased a revolving drum type of picker in the early 50s but only used it to remove a few of the feathers on the turkeys' backs and necks where the picker didn't leave blemishes. We learned of a system developed by the Pickwick Company. After considerable deliberation we bought one of their systems, which included a scalder and track. With this system the turkeys needed to be fully cooled in ice water and when removed from the ice water sealed in a plastic bag. It was a significant change from our previous methods but decreased labor costs. We were concerned whether the consumer would readily accept our product in a plastic bag but the change was met with approval.

Cooling the turkeys in ice water rather than refrigerated air required the purchase of an ice machine. Money was always a scarce commodity so the ice machine we purchased was smaller than desirable. Weekends, when we weren't processing, we regularly emptied the ice machine's storage bin and rolled tanks of ice into the freezer to be used the next week. At holiday time we sent our truck to an ice plant, and brought back tons of ice in 300 pound cakes, which we stored in our freezer until needed. For many years I handled large cakes of

(above) Dry picking the turkey legs before scalding the turkey. The legs would skin and look bad if they were picked after scalding. Roland Victory is the man on the left.

(below) Circa 1960 photo of Chuck Green scalding a turkey to loosen its feathers, which were then removed by hand.

ice with ice tongs similar to the ice man of a century ago.

As we increased our efficiency in removing feathers from the turkeys, we also moved to reduce the effort and time catching turkeys and bringing them to the processing plant. We converted an old garage, next to where the turkeys were killed, into a live holding area. Now we could drive the turkeys directly from both the pastures and the pole barns to the processing plant without having to catch them. Next we constructed a platform in the killing area so the turkeys could be driven up a ramp, convenient to the person doing the killing. This eliminated the previously needed crates and the extra handling of the turkeys.

About 1960, the City of Syracuse passed an ordinance requiring the inspection of all processing facilities whose products were sold in the city. Since we sold turkeys directly to stores, restaurants, hotels and at the Regional Market, all in Syracuse, we had to comply. Numerous small chicken and turkey producers could not comply and went out of business. We made the necessary changes, including testing our water every three months, and continued in business. Syracuse continued this program until an inspection program was initiated by New York State. When New York State took over the inspection we were required to have a State inspector, not only check our facilities but also inspect each individual bird.

I had been considering further processing some of our turkeys for several years to even out our production cycle and to market each turkey profitably whenever it was sold. I had no idea how to begin as I had never boned a turkey or seen one boned. I learned of a Cornell Cooperative Extension agent on Long Island who was teaching some of the growers in Suffolk County how to bone turkeys and made arrangements to have him show me how to bone a turkey. I came back home, boned a few turkeys, seasoned the meat, stuffed it in a casing and cooked it in our Cryovac shrink tank. Next, I put the turkey roll in a box with some napkins and a knife and made some sales calls in the Syracuse area. It was delicious but most people had never seen a turkey roll before and were hesitant to order

A circa 1970 photo of boneless breasts and turkey rolls that have just come from out of the ovens.

Circa 1964 photo of Bob Bitz checking the temperature of turkey rolls. The turkey rolls were wrapped in aluminum foil and cooked five nights a week in pizza ovens. They were repackaged in clear film Cryovac bags while the meat was still warm.

them. My first success was with the manager of the Howard Johnson's Restaurant at DeWitt, who was using turkey rolls furnished by the company. Although he was not supposed to purchase turkey except from their commissary, he bought some from me and I was in the turkey further processing business.

I had been told that the Sky Chef Restaurant used large whole turkeys so I paid them a visit to sell some of our large toms. They told me that they wanted to get away from whole turkeys and were interested in finding a source of raw boneless breasts. I responded, "Let me see what I can do." Back at the farm, I boned the breast of a large tom, used white butcher string to hold the two halves tightly together and went back to Sky Chefs. They roasted the breast and were pleased, ordering eight for the following week. This started a relationship that lasted as long as they operated in Syracuse. It

was also a product that we sold to numerous other restaurants and universities as long as we were in business. Over the years we probably sold several hundred thousand tied breasts as the result of filling the needs of one customer. We also produced smaller tied breasts from hen turkeys that were very popular for retail sale.

Our first delivery truck was very crude. It was our farm truck with a stake rack body, which we used to draw feed, fertilizer and everything else of any size that needed to be moved on the highway. The turkeys and turkey products were covered with a tarpaulin which we pulled back whenever we made a delivery. Our first delivery vehicle was a Chevrolet Corvan that was enclosed and provided convenient access for loading and delivering. I was proud and pleased to have that to replace our stake rack truck, which we continued to use for large whole turkey deliveries a number of years.

Bob with our first turkey delivery truck. It wasn't refrigerated but was an improvement over the stake rack farm truck for delivering turkey products.

Our Cryovac bag sales representative told me of a turkey roll, roasted in an oven rather than cooked in water, that was excellent and being successfully marketed in the Boston area. He arranged for me to make a visit to the company and observe their process. It was definitely a superior product and we started producing a similar one. We bought a small two-deck commercial oven and started producing roasted turkey rolls. By this time there were a number of turkey rolls on the market but none of them approached the quality of these.

We developed delivery routes for Wednesday and Thursday of each week and each day, while delivering, I attempted to stop and see at least two potential customers. I carried a turkey roll, knife and napkins. Amazingly we obtained a new customer on about half of the calls. Demand required we add a further processing room to the dressing plant and buy an additional larger oven. One of the secrets was slow roasting.

For twenty years, one of my jobs was to put the rolls in the ovens at night and check them at 6:00 a.m. to have them ready for packaging when the workers arrived at 8:00.

The success of the turkey rolls and the tied breasts created many problems. Although there was good demand for the breasts and part of the thighs, few of the drumsticks, wings, necks and giblets were being marketed. These items needed to be sold to obtain optimum profits. We were able to sell the necks and giblets to mink farmers for a few cents a pound. We managed to sell drumsticks, wings and surplus thighs to retail stores to use as loss leaders. They didn't bring as large a return as we wished but it was a way to dispose of them. Dr. Robert Baker of Cornell was a good friend and helped me develop a variety of products using these parts. The products were good but none of them were a real success. We were ahead of our time and customers were not ready to buy turkey in unusual forms. It would have taken a large advertising budget to break through this barrier. It wasn't until the 1990s that we were able to utilize these items effectively.

We were believers in the old adage, "waste not, want not," which made it difficult for us to throw away good turkey carcasses. Whenever we had a turkey at home, my mother always used the carcass to make delicious turkey soup. We tried numerous recipes and decided to market turkey rice soup. It was good but we lacked the volume for successful promotion and discontinued producing it after a couple of years.

The successful sale of our turkey rolls required that they be produced 52 weeks of the year to supply our customers. Our farm labor force had been just Dad, myself and two hired men, except at holiday time when neighbors helped us. I contacted some of these neighbors and was able to employ three to work as needed. They started working only a few hours a week but were soon working three or four days a week. With my meager skills I taught them how to bone turkeys, tie breasts and do all of the other necessary tasks. As the business expanded we extended their hours and added another person when more help was needed. Soon their skills were superior to mine. I was in the plant almost every morning for an hour or two and usually there an hour near the end of their day.

Over the years we gradually increased the number of our turkey flocks and extended our slaughtering season into the spring and earlier in the fall. Even so, it was necessary to freeze enough turkeys to last from April to September. When we ran out of freezer room we rented space in Syracuse Cold Storage and at times had to buy turkeys from other sources. I hated to do this as the quality seldom was equal to our birds.

One of the additional sources of income from our turkeys, since the 1930s, was the sale of white turkey feathers. We saved both the large quill

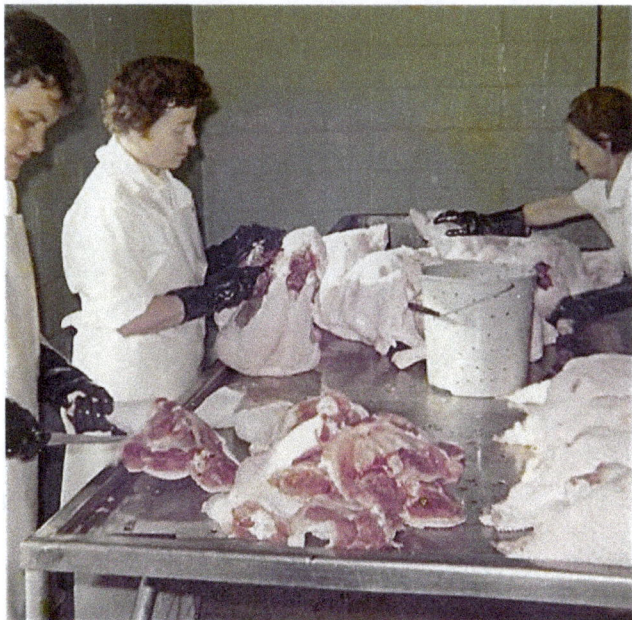

Circa 1964 photo of Phyllis Ellis, Alice Warner and Rose McGovern boning turkeys for turkey rolls.

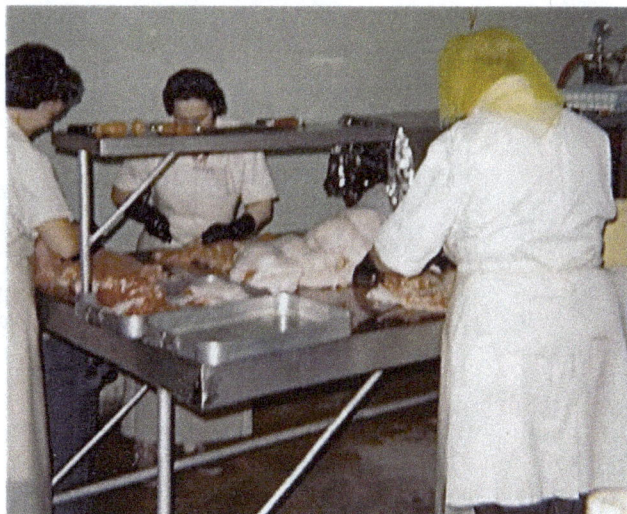

Connie Smith, Rose Dodge and Ida Roth trimming turkey meat that will be wrapped in aluminum foil for roasting.

A circa 1955 photo of dressed turkeys, hanging from an overhead trolly, in the new cooler.

A 1960s photo of a flock of turkeys on the Wilson farm. Notice the two tall light poles. We put several poles with lights around the roosts to deter predators. We no longer had anyone sleep with the turkeys at night. Even though this flock was 1,500 feet from the processing plant we drove the turkeys to the processing plant rather than catching them.

feathers and the smaller body feathers. It took the person killing the turkeys extra time but paid well. Although half of our turkeys in 1959 were still bronze with feathers of no value, we sold 4,000 pounds of feathers from about 6,000 white turkeys.

There was opportunity for very rapid growth during the 1960s but because we chose not to borrow money we grew slowly. In retrospect I am very happy that we took this path. A few turkey farms in the United States grew rapidly and were successful but the majority were forced out of business because they overextended. Some years were better than others but we always were able to show a profit.

In the 60s, too many turkeys were produced and many growers lost money. Some wanted the US government to establish a marketing order to limit the number of turkeys each grower could produce. There were several hearings and I attended the one for the northeast held in Albany and testified against a marketing order. Fortunately for our operation,

I was successful and we were able to continue the gradual growth of our turkey business.

About 1960 it became apparent that we needed some office help. My wife, Janice, called our store and restaurant customers by telephone every Monday morning, answered phone calls and waited on retail customers. I kept the books and my mother took care of the banking. Because family had always tended to the office aspects of the business, it seemed like a big move to bring someone in from the outside to do much of this work. We advertised and were fortunate to hire Helen Carpenter who was our total office staff for several years and continued in the office until she retired in about 1985. She always joked with me because when she first started I suggested she bring a book with her to read in her spare time. She never had any spare time! Her day off, besides Sunday, was Tuesday so she could be there on Saturday when a greater number of retail customers came to the farm.

Turkeys on range in the 50s. It was difficult for the turkeys to keep from losing weight when outside in the winter. Note the catching cage on the left. There is a fence around an area that is large enough to hold about 200 turkeys. About 20 were driven into the telescoping cage ending in a large box with hinged doors on top. The men could then reach down and easily catch the turkeys by their legs.

We were fortunate to have fine people come to work with us. We attempted to treat them like family and most of the ones employed through the 60s stayed with us for many years. By 1961, we were producing 16,000 turkeys a year and the number almost doubled to 30,000 by 1966. The number of employees reached a dozen with a full-time delivery person and a supervisor in the processing plant. We had previously instituted a profit sharing plan for our full-time employees, gave them personal time and sick days with pay as well as their birthday. It was a tradition for my mother to come

This is a picture of Janice Bitz with a group of visiting schoolchildren. Janice took many thousands of children on tours of the turkey farm. Each child went home with an apple, a pencil and some feathers.

to the processing plant with a pail of coffee and cookies each morning at 10:00. The coffee and cookies continued after my mother fell in the plant and broke her hip one day. However, the coffee continued, but was made by one of the employees on site.

As the turkey business expanded, our retail sales increased at the farm. When people came to the farm to buy a turkey, since we lived only 100 feet away, Janice went to the small retail sales area in processing plant to wait on them. She also gave many tours of the farm to schoolchildren during the fall, eventually more than 2,000 children a year. This was good public relations and spread the word about the farm. During the early years of the tours, Janice took the children into the processing plant where they saw the turkeys being prepared for market, a part of the tour which we later discontinued. Times were changing and some of the public felt it inappropriate for children to be exposed to turkeys being processed.

A circa 1960 photo of Bob Bitz in the 1949 freezer with some large frozen tom turkeys. Two large tom turkeys, for sale to restaurants, were in each wooden crate.

A 1954 photo of Plainville Turkey Farm. The building under construction in the background is a 48 x 168 brooder house, the first large turkey growing building on the farm.

30

A beautiful flock of bronze toms in the early 1960s ready for marketing. Plainville and the entire turkey industry moved from bronze to white turkeys in the 1960s, only because the dark pinfeathers of the bronze did not look desirable to the consumer.

A 1960s photo of some Plainville team members enjoying coffee and cookies during the middle of the morning.

A flock of turkeys on range in the early 1960s. The range was a fine place to grow turkeys when the weather was good, if you could keep disease and varmints away from the turkeys.

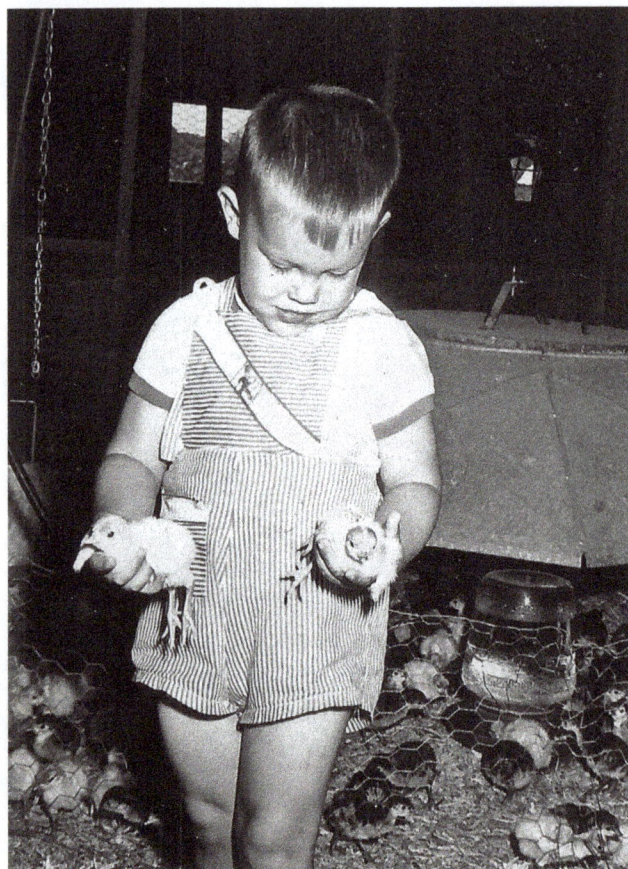

Mark Bitz holding two baby turkeys.

Some ribbons won by Plainville turkeys from the New York State Fair in 1938 and 1953, one ribbon from a New York State show and two from National Turkey Federation shows.

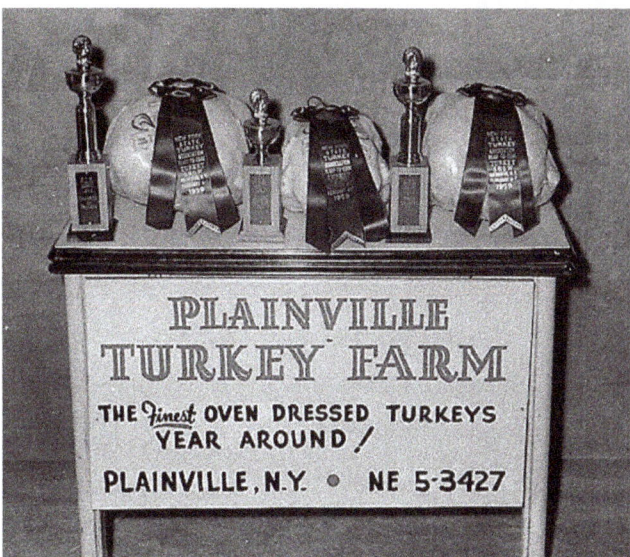

Circa 1958 trophies won in a NYS dressed turkey show. It is always good to compare your products with the competition to help you constantly improve.

A circa 1964 photo of a bucket elevator being raised on the Wilson farm. It was used to put corn in the nearby grain bins.

1966 to 1985

By 1966, the herd of Guernsey cows, potatoes, beans and cabbage were all history. Turkeys had become our total source of income and even the corn, oats and wheat that we grew, were for the benefit of the turkeys.

Our children, Cynthia, Mark and Bruce had become not only part of our family but also part of our farm family. They were given chores and helped their parents and grandparents whenever they could. Cynthia, the oldest, accompanied me whenever it was safe for her and when she could help. When each of the boys became three, each of them were with me much of the time. One of the children's' first chores was to help drive turkeys and help take care of the baby poults.

My dad was semi retired by 1966 and for several years had left the decision making up to me. He still delivered turkey rolls each week, in our station wagon, to a customer in Utica and one in Canton even though we had a regular driver with a refrigerated truck. Dad kept a team of workhorses on the farm until about this time and used one of them to cultivate the garden. Both my dad and mother remained keenly interested in the business and mother made a weekly trip to the bank with the receipts.

In 1968, we were producing turkalona, a product similar to bologna, turkaloaf, turkey burgers, soup and gravy. We had high hopes for each of these products but only turkey gravy met our sales expectations. Dr. Baker, a poultry product specialist at Cornell, had helped us with the meat products and Alice Warner, who was a valued employee for many years, developed the soup and the gravy. We discovered that very few people liked to make gravy when they cooked a whole turkey, and their gravy was often of poor quality. Sales of gravy were not large at first but increased each year we were in business.

Before we made gravy, we sold a product called turkey juice. When we roasted turkey rolls they lost almost 20% of their weight from the juices that came from them as they cooked. We packaged these juices in quart containers, froze them and sold the juices to hospitals and retail customers. Many people used these juices for making soup and gravy. As our gravy sales increased, we discontinued selling turkey juice. Because we served a number of hospitals, we also made turkey rolls without any added salt. The hospitals and nursing homes purchased the juice that came from these rolls made without salt.

Another unusual product we sold for many years was turkey pieces. Because we had no use for the carcass other than making soup, we used a knife to cut small pieces of meat from the carcass after it had been boned. These pieces were packaged in seven pound bags and frozen. Hospitals and institutions used these to make inexpensive turkey entrees. Eventually a small circular electric knife was used to remove more meat than we could economically remove by hand.

Wanting to utilize as much of the turkey as possible, we decided to sell turkey fries. These were the testicles from large toms that we packaged in pint containers and frozen. Unfortunately only an occasional customer who had the urge for exotic

An aerial view of the main farm about 1967. Since the processing plant was constructed in 1950 there had been three additions, the old tobacco shed and cow barn have been torn down and a farm shop constructed. (Dark green building in the center.)

A circa 1970 photo of our first moving line for eviscerating turkeys. Previously eviceration had been done on tables but when individual bird inspection was required by New York State we went to a moving line. New York State meat inspector Robert Dingman is in the center of the photo. I bought this processing line, for just a few dollars, from a chicken plant in Southern New York that had gone out of business.

food bought them and we discontinued packaging them.

Because we were growing more corn, oats and wheat as well as producing more turkeys and increasing turkey further processing, my responsibilities increased to a point that my health was affected. Dust especially bothered me. We searched for a farm manager and in 1969 John Murch, who had grown up on a turkey farm in MA, joined us. John took over the responsibilities involved in growing the turkeys and the crops. This allowed me to get away from most of the dust and to spend more time in processing and marketing. John was a fine hard working man and was with us for about 20 years.

The following year, New York State took over the inspection of meat and poultry processing plants, which included individual bird inspection. In anticipation of this change, as well as the need for larger processing facilities, we constructed a major addition to our processing plant. As part of this expansion we bought a used overhead track conveying system and eviscerated the turkeys on a moving line rather than on tables as had done in the past. The employees were very apprehensive

concerning this change but were soon pleased with the results. The state inspector examined each turkey, and one of our employees by his side, removed any blemish or part that was damaged. We always had an excellent relationship with the inspectors, partially because our standards were higher than those required by the State. New York State had two inspectors that rotated, alternating one month at a time. Interestingly one of the State inspectors, Bob Dingman, became a federal inspector when we changed over to federal inspection in 1975. He continued as federal inspector on our farm until he retired in 1990.

I knew that eventually, when our business grew to the point that we sold products in other states, federal inspection would be required. Before we made the addition to the processing plant I flew to Philadelphia, the nearest federal district meat and poultry office, to have them look over our plans to make sure our plant would comply when we had future federal inspection. The addition to the plant included a freezer where we stacked up to 15,000 turkeys, similar to stacking cordwood. When we were processing live turkeys, other than at holiday time, we dressed 400 a day, boning half

A pile of thousands of frozen turkeys in one of our freezers. Until we were able to have live turkeys available for further processing 52 weeks a year we had to store turkeys for further processing when we did not have live turkeys large enough to market. Each day, when we were processing a sufficient number of turkeys, we piled 100 to 200 so they could freeze before we piled more the next day. When we removed the turkeys we placed them in large chill tanks and thawed them in water.

Charles Pickard Jr. (Butch) and Mark Bitz filling a store order for fresh Thanksgiving turkeys. We used white boxes with red lettering until about 1990. We changed to earth tones when we decided to feed our turkeys all natural feeds.

of them and freezing the other half. As the further processing portion of our business increased, we ordered poults that were all toms. The toms grew to a larger size and could be further processed more efficiently. By 1972, three-quarters of our turkeys were toms.

With the increase in the numbers of turkeys we grew, along with the extended growing season, we needed to find an alternative source of day old poults. It was important that the poults be of high quality and disease free. We found a well operated company in Michigan and one in North Carolina, the Goldsboro Milling Company that supplied us with poults for many years.

There was an unexpected bonus when we changed our poult suppliers. The poults from Goldsboro were much easier to brood and had stronger legs, which is especially critical when growing large toms. Both livability and feed conversion improved. There was also a savings in labor because the poults came to the farm already debeaked and with the snoods removed from the

tom turkeys. For almost 20 years we had used an electric knife to debeak the turkeys when they were four weeks of age. Turkeys like to peck at almost anything and sometimes at each other. With the end of the upper beak removed they couldn't pull another turkey's feathers as well. All turkeys have a fleshy snood on top of their heads that is purely ornamental. The snood expands and hangs down several inches from on one side of a tom's head when he is strutting. While fighting, toms seem to love to take hold of their opponent's snood. There was concern that erysipelas was spread through damaged snoods and they were removed for that reason. Removing the snoods of the day old poults was similar to hulling strawberries; poult in one hand, snood between thumb and forefinger and then a quick pull.

In 1970, we were producing 45,000 turkeys a year and had 20 employees. About half of the turkeys were grown on pasture and the remaining were grown in the 11 buildings we had constructed. We were gradually moving away from growing

Another large corn bin being constructed next to the old tobacco warehouse that we converted into a granary. The tobacco shed that had been converted into large corn cribs is on the left. In another few years both of these buildings became outdated and were torn down to make room for modern and labor efficient replacements.

turkeys on pasture because of our extended growing season when the weather was not suitable for growing turkeys outside.

November with its Thanksgiving holiday was by far our largest sales month of the year. Each year the chain stores offered frozen turkeys as loss leaders at ridiculously low prices. Sometimes they even gave them away with other purchases. This was tough competition. Although we were always concerned how our sales would be affected, each year we were pleased that customers were willing to pay the relatively high price for our fresh turkeys. We were retailing our turkeys for 79 cents a pound, two or three times the price of the loss leaders. We always strongly encouraged our wholesale customers to retail our turkeys for at least our retail price.

A popular holiday product that we developed in the early 70s was a stuffed and seasoned frozen ready to cook turkey. The consumer placed the frozen turkey in the oven, in the bag it came in. It had to be cooked slowly and the bottom of the bag opened automatically during the roasting process.

There was a pop-up thermometer in the turkey that indicated when the turkey was fully cooked. In 1972, we produced 1,500 of these turkeys. It was popular but we discontinued it a few years later because of the potential food poisoning, if the consumer didn't closely follow cooking and handling instructions. The stuffing in the turkey could serve as an ideal medium for bacterial growth. We continued to market stuffing but in aluminum containers that could be heated separately from the turkey.

Our first long term employee, Charles Green, came to work on the farm in 1946 after serving in World War II. He was a valued employee who retired in about 1983. His wife, Nellie, helped us dress turkeys in the early 50s, and was one of the first employees to work in further processing. She worked until she retired, which was about a year after her husband. Their youngest daughter, Ann, worked on the farm from 1978 until the business was sold in 2007. Chuck and Nellie's other three children also helped, but for shorter periods of

39

Bruce Bitz in a building of 10 week old turkeys. Both Mark and Bruce, when they were about 12, had the responsibility of growing a flock of several thousand turkeys.

time. They were a fine family and lived across the road from Janice and I.

Another early employee was Arthur Kinney who joined us in 1956 and stayed until he retired in about 1990. Art's wife, Sally, also worked for us for more than a decade before her untimely death. Some of our other long term early employees, who helped dress turkeys and worked in further processing, were Rose McGovern, Ida Roth, Rose Dodge, Mary Nipper, Janice Congdon, Kate Bennett, Janice Kline and Pat Castiglia. They all worked for more than 10 years, with Rose Dodge, Mary, both Janices and Pat working well over 20 years. Janice Kline worked a number of years in quality control, even coming back to help us at Thanksgiving and Christmas for several years after she retired. All of these ladies began working at the farm before 1977 and were wonderful and dedicated people to work with. They were as proud of the products we produced as I was!

In approximately 1969, I approached our neighbor and good friend Allen Bratt to see if he would be willing to start day old poults for us on a year around basis. He said he would and we constructed an 8,000 square foot brooding building on his farm. About five flocks of turkeys were started each year and moved either to our growing buildings or pasture at eight weeks of age. This worked very well for us as it allowed us to start poults in an area totally removed from the larger turkeys and minimize potential disease problems. Allen was a conscientious and dedicated man who consistently produced excellent turkeys. Allen's son, Doug, also helped him care for the turkeys.

Brooding the poults away from the main farm worked so well that in 1982 we bought another farm two miles from our main farm and built a 16,000 square foot brooder building to start day old poults. Fred Mercer took care of this building until Allen Bratt joined us as a full-time team member in

1984, after turning his farm over to his son Doug. Our term of lease was completed for the building on Allen's farm and Doug was able to convert it to use for his dairy cattle.

A valued employee who came to the farm in 1971 and had many areas of responsibility was Bill Rogers. His first job was helping build a pole barn and afterwards helped on the farm and processing plant in a variety of jobs before delivering our turkey products. Later he oversaw deliveries and then moved into sales. He worked in sales until the turkey operation was sold in 2007 and is still is a key member of the marketing team at Hains Celestial who are now growing and marketing Plainville turkeys. Gene Ellis also started working with us directly from high school in 1971 and worked on the farm and feed mill from 1971 to about 1991. Interestingly, both men while working on the farm met their future wives who were also working on the farm.

Until 1978, we did most of our building construction with our farm employees and supplemented with high school or college students during the summer. While Mark Bitz was home from college in the summer he headed up the construction of this building.

We had a number of fine young men who worked on the farm during their summer vacations from high school and college. They did a variety of tasks but often helped build a pole barn during the summer. One of the first was Ed Bratt and a year or two later his brother Gary, both brothers of Nelson Bratt who joined us full-time in 1977. Craig Oakes and Gene Lynch also helped, along with Gene's sister Wendy who helped take care of our children when they were little and waited on customers in the salesroom.

My sons, Mark and Bruce and daughter Cynthia also worked summers as well as at holidays and other times during the year. Both of my boys raised about 10 pigs, as a learning experience, when they were 11. When each one was 12, he had the responsibility for growing a flock of 3,000 turkeys from day old to market. I felt that it would provide them the opportunity both to learn and handle responsibility. Each one performed well.

Long term employees coming to the farm in 1977 and 1978 were Beverley McKalsen, Lois Monica, Roxanne Webster, Luis Forres, Charmaine Cole and Nelson Bratt. Charmaine still works for Hains, in our former cooking plant at Liverpool, and Nelson continues to be a valued team member for my son Mark at Central New York Feeds. Nelson was responsible for growing our turkeys, reaching 800,000 a year in 2007. He was extremely conscientious and produced the best turkeys in the country.

Until the late 70s, when Steve Hunsinger joined us, we never had a team member for full-time maintenance and repair of machinery, equipment and buildings. Until then, we used the limited skills of each team member and hired a variety of businesses with skilled trades to work as needed. We often had to wait for an emergency repair because of the lack of a person with those skills. Steve

George Jewell hanging live turkeys circa 1970. George was a retired railroad employee who was past 70 and worked part time hanging live turkeys. We tried to tell him it was too hard for someone his age but he insisted he wanted to do it.

This is a circa 1975 photo of the annual farm picnic for team members and their families on Bob and Janice Bitz's front lawn. Plenty of food, games and prizes were the order of the day.

Five long term turkey processing employees being honored. From left to right Connie Smith, Ida Roth, Mary Nipper, Rose Dodge and Nellie Green.

Four long time Plainville employees being honored. Left to right Mary Nipper, Alice Warner, Bill Rogers and Janice Congdon. Some twenty-five years later, in 2007, when the turkey business was sold, the ladies had retired but Bill Rogers was still a valued team member and continued working for the new owners.

was a great asset and we sorely missed him with his untimely passing in 1993. As the years passed we gradually employed more knowledgable people for maintenance and repairs.

Another step forward in 1982 was establishing a second shift to clean the processing plant after each day's work. Previously, at the end of the day, everyone in the processing plant spent about the last half hour of their day cleaning the plant. At the end of the day everyone was anxious to go home and the cleaning wasn't always as thorough as desired. Dan McKalsen, who came to work with us in 1982, led this crew for a number of years. As our production increased, the night cleanup crew became a necessary part of our operation.

In 1981, Janice Shader joined us part-time in our small retail salesroom in the dressing plant. When we moved our retail sales to a separate new building on the farm she did a fine job managing that, along with our new visitor center. The following year Judy Hunsinger came to work

in the processing plant and later she became an important part of our office sales staff. Art Bratt, a fine young neighbor who had discontinued dairy farming became one of our turkey growers for 15 years until his early death. Art's father Maynard who had also retired from dairying joined us in 1984 and delivered turkey products to customers until he retired in 1993.

Our intent always, was to treat our team members as we would like to be treated. Because of this we were able to hire and keep people that accepted responsibility for doing their work well and producing excellent products. I tried to work with our team members whenever I could and keep them informed of what was happening throughout the business. Until about 1980, there was a broad interaction of all team members with those in the processing plant who came outside to help drive turkeys and the ones on the farm coming inside the plant to help process turkeys during extremely busy times. We tried to pay a reasonable wage but it was

43

A circa 1975 photograph of Bob Bitz on the roof of the processing plant, as a new ice machine is being set into place. This was a big advancement as we often purchased ice because our existing two smaller ice machines were unable to produce enough.

A circa 1975 photo of eviscerated turkeys cooling in tanks of ice water. Compressed air was used to agitate the water and cool the turkeys more rapidly. Tons of ice had to be shoveled and needed to be replenished as it melted. A few years later we purchased a huge continuous chiller that eliminated the tanks and shoveling ice.

This is our feed mill on the Wilson farm circa 1975. There are four load out bins that each held six ton of feed, in front of the center of the red barn. There was a Mix-Mill inside the barn, with adjustable settings, that ground and mixed four separate ingredients to make the appropriate feed for each age of turkeys. The white tank in front of the red barn held heated animal fat that was added to the feed going through the Mix-Mill to make the feed more palatable and provide extra energy in the feed rations.

always less than I would have liked. About 1967, we set up a profit sharing plan for our team members and for at least five years were able to make the maximum contribution permitted by federal law. We continued to make contributions each year but there were years when it was less than we would have desired.

By 1975 we were growing 75,000 turkeys a year, which was now half of the turkeys produced in New York State, compared to less than one-half of one percent 30 years earlier. We also started producing turkey hot dogs and turkey salami, but neither product proved to be successful. This was the year of the changeover from New York inspection to inspection by the USDA. We could now sell our turkeys and turkey products anyplace in the US but only a small portion of our production went out of the state for more than a decade.

To obtain the maximum return for our turkeys, we were constantly attempting to add value to our products. In 1973, we had opened a restaurant at Cicero and in 1976, now that we had USDA inspection, we started a mail order business that offered customers smoked whole turkeys, cooked whole turkeys and smoked turkey breasts. We employed an advertising agency to develop a mail order catalog and do advertising for our mail order products. Our turkeys traveled to all corners of the country but less than 1,000 were sold that year.

I had purchased the farm and business from my parents in 1968, paying them over a period of years. In about 1976 I borrowed outside money, for the first time, to help expand our business. Buildings and equipment for growing turkeys, operating a feed mill, processing and marketing turkeys and growing crops required a great deal of capital. Whenever we increased the size of our business, in one of these segments, capital was necessary to expand each of the others. Our profits were becoming inadequate to fuel a continued 6-10% increase in volume each year. The Farm Credit System provided us additional capital but we borrowed at a safe level to avoid an adverse situation that might put the farm in jeopardy.

In 1977, our annual production hit 100,000 turkeys and our sales passed $1 million. We employed Linda Cline as a part-time marketing person, the first person other than myself to spend much time increasing sales. Later, Linda became marketing manager and helped broaden the breadth of sales through advertising, public relations and personal contact. Until this time, because of our unwillingness to expand with borrowed money, we often had to tell a potential customer that we couldn't supply them but would try to have enough product for them the following year.

During the first few years of further processing we were forced to say no to some potentially large buyers because we felt that we could not properly supply them. It was in about 1977 that Wegman Markets wanted to order more than I was able to supply without affecting our existing customers.

We made each new building more labor efficient and better looking. These two buildings were constructed on the main farm about 1975. Feed was delivered by a truck and blown into a bin that kept feed in front of the turkeys at all times. Curtains, operated by a hand winch were on both sides of the buildings to permit natural air flow.

In about 1979, four tractor trailers arrived with materials for three large growing buildings. It was following the first energy crisis and we attempted to make the buildings 'green' before the expression was even used. There were no windows in the buildings and they were well insulated.

Bruce and Bob Bitz, in 1972, posing for a newspaper photographer and receiving a little free publicity for Plainville turkeys. It was the week before Thanksgiving but the snow came early that year.

Driving turkeys toward the processing plant. By driving a small flock in front, the ones behind followed more easily. One time when driving turkeys, Lou Bitz, who had cared for them regularly, walked ahead and the turkeys followed right along behind her.

They became very upset and wouldn't buy any product from us for more than a decade. Some years later, Wegman's became our largest customer and we had an outstanding relationship with them.

When I think of Wegmans , I often think back to 1958 when we used my mother's old vacuum cleaner to remove air from the turkey bags before shrinking the bag tightly around the bird in a hot water dip tank. I wanted to replace the vacuum cleaner with a more effective Cryovac vacuum machine but it cost more than I was willing to pay. An over enthusiastic Cryovac Company sales representative had sold Wegman's two of these vacuum machines but they were using only one and wanted to sell the surplus machine. I made a deal to swap some frozen turkeys for Wegman's extra machine, which was a winner for both of us.

One of the products that we started to produce in the 70s was turkey ham. We trimmed and cured turkey thighs to produce this product. To my amazement, when we cooked the thighs, we had an excellent turkey ham that looked and tasted like pork ham. Its fat content was lower than pork ham and it became quite popular with consumers who were oriented toward healthy eating. It was a labor intensive product to produce but provided a good use for many of our surplus thighs.

In 1978, our farm was honored by the New York State Agricultural Society as a Century Farm. The farm had been started by my great-great grandfather in 1835 and my mother was especially pleased that our farm was recognized. That year we remodeled our small sales area in the processing plant. It was not large but had a small freezer and cooler where some of our products could be displayed for customers. It also separated the sales area from the processing area. When we made this change, my good friend Herb Hildebrandt installed a speaker that gobbled like a turkey every time a customer came into the salesroom. The gobbling was a recording Herb and I had obtained earlier from some of our live turkey toms.

As the business increased in size we needed a knowledgable person as our processing plant manager. Since our operation was small, we were unable to attract a proven plant manager. In 1980, John Amos, a young man from Virginia who had grown up in the poultry business, joined us as plant manager. John served us as plant manager until 1989 when he moved into marketing.

Many changes continued to happen in 1980 and 1981. We printed a small recipe book for customers, opened a restaurant on Erie Blvd. in Syracuse, installed a computer and made a major addition to our processing plant. This addition included a new killing and picking area with an overhead line and automatic pickers that permitted us to kill and eviscerate 600 turkeys an hour with only 18 employees involved in that part of the operation. We were not growing enough turkeys to use the new addition many hours a week but it did provide opportunity to grow our business and increase our fresh turkey sales at Thanksgiving time. We had 20 large pole buildings to house our turkeys at this time and 50 employees. We were now further processing two-thirds of the turkeys we grew and a number of our team members were working full-time in further processing.

The farm and feed portions of our business needed to change along with the turkey sales. In 1979, our corn production increased to 700 acres and in the early 80s we started roasting whole soybeans to use in our turkey feed. Soybeans are high in protein and in fat but an enzyme, that is a deterrent to turkey growth, needs to be subjected to a high temperature before soybeans can be used for turkey feed.

By 1984 we were growing 200,000 turkeys a year. This was two-thirds of the turkeys produced in New York. We were also producing apple and pumpkin pies at the farm. We bought whole northern spy apples and peeled them to make the apple pies. The pies were excellent and well liked but our production methods were not efficient and after a few years we discontinued production. We also produced some Canadian style bacon from turkey thighs and made a taco filling but neither of these items achieved sufficient volume to continue their production more than a few years.

In June of 1985 we celebrated the 150th anniversary of our family farm. We invited customers, suppliers and friends to the farm for festivities and a tour. It was well received and created a good amount of publicity. A turkey cookbook was also prepared and a copy given to each of our guests.

The farm had come a long way since 1835 with change occurring more rapidly each year. From a labor intensive farm with only family and one or two hired men for over 100 years it was now a highly mechanized farm with 60 employees and a variety of high quality turkey products marketed throughout New York.

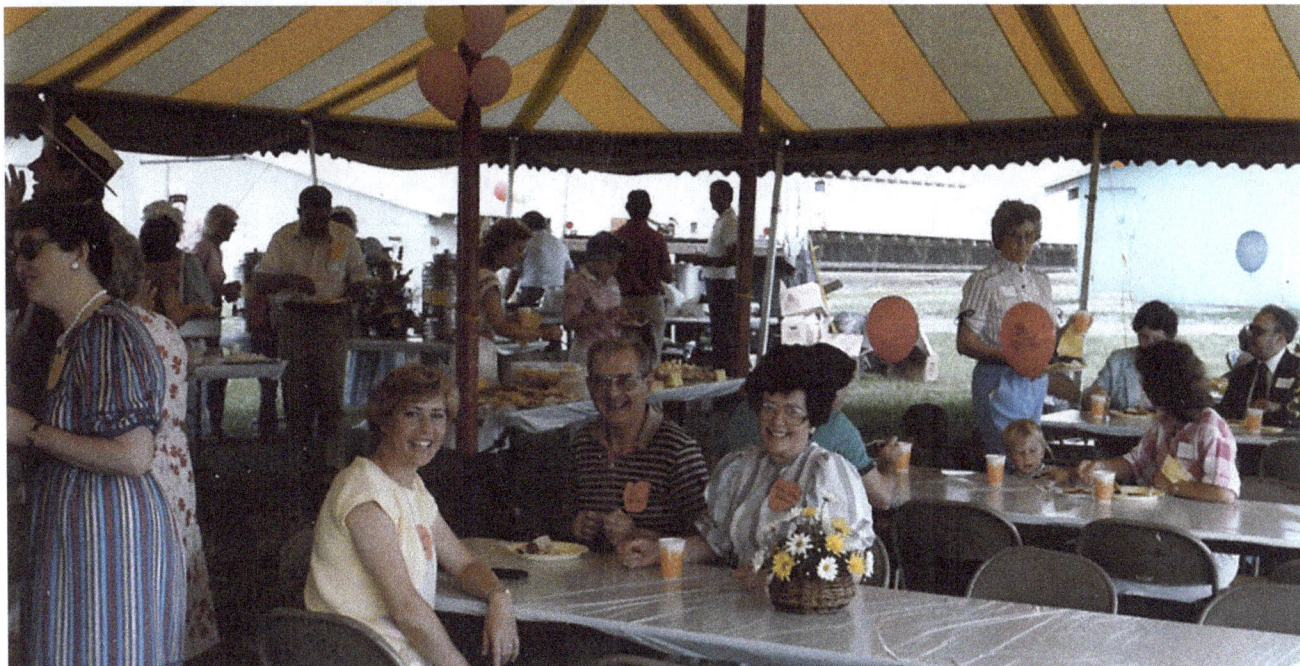

Festivities at the celebration of the 150th year of the farm in our family.

Team members names were put in a hat and two lucky people went for a ride in a hot air balloon at the annual picnic.

The 150th anniversary of the farm was held in the summer of 1985 with many guests coming for food and entertainment.

The perfect phone for taking turkey orders at Plainville Turkey Farm!

Family members attending the 150th anniversary of the farm were Metta Bitz, Ruth Bitz Dettbarn, Janice Bitz, Rebecca Bowen, Bob Bitz, Cynthia Bitz Bowen and Sean Bowen.

Two big turkeys! The turkey costume was made for special events and parades, to help promote Plainville turkey. It was a fun costume but terribly hot on a warm day.

A Career Day exhibit at Cornell University that Bob was invited to for several years around 1970. My statement, "Poultry, the Meat of the Future" has become fact, as poultry consumption has surpassed both beef and pork.

A 1996 photo of Bob Bitz with his grandsons, Karl and Asher Bitz, getting ready to have a picture taken for use as the image for a new farm logo.

FIVE

1985 to 1995

Not only did we celebrate the 150th anniversary of our farm in 1985 but the sixth generation to operate it came back to the farm. After graduating from high school, Mark spent three years at Purdue earning his BS in agricultural economics. Following graduation he spent a year in Poland teaching English and working on a state owned farm, under the auspices of the Church of the Brethren. Conditions were extremely difficult in Poland as they were indirectly controlled by the Soviets. Mark had an unusual experience spending the year without the niceties of life that we take for-granted in the US, and living under Soviet style socialism.

He returned from Poland and took three years of graduate work at Cornell, completing his Master's and the course work for his doctorate. In 1985, he decided to return to the farm. Mark became Vice President of the farm and general manager. He had worked on the farm during vacations when he wasn't traveling, and I had always kept him informed regarding what was happening on the farm.

During the continuing growth of the farm business, I had often wished that I had knowledgable people for consultation in helping make long term business decisions. I had spent my years at Cornell planning to come back to the farm and continuing it as a family farm. Had I realized the business was going to grow as extensively, I might have chosen some different courses.

In 1985, I formed a farm advisory board consisting of a banker, Bill Stevens, a businessman,

Dick Call and a poultry professor, Joe Regenstein. Mark and I met with them quarterly at the farm and found their wisdom and experience helpful. Bill Stevens moved to the Albany area about a year later and Doug Brodie replaced him. Our advisory committee continued until about 1993. Mark was doing a fine job as General Manager so I decided he should be President of the corporation. This enabled him to become a member of the Young Presidents Organization (YPO). He also became a member of a Central New York forum of eight YPO members and this forum served as an advisory group for each of its members.

Any business has a myriad of challenges, many arising unexpectedly from day to day and well beyond the scope of good planning or the help of an advisory board. One of the most annoying problems was breast meat that turned pink when it was cooked. There was nothing wrong with the meat but customers thought it was not fully cooked. For a long time we did not understand all the causes of this problem, which was a completely unacceptable situation to the buyers for large chains. Some other turkey processors also sporadically had this problem. Eventually, after a number of years, we discovered that naturally occurring nitrates in the water, bacteria and the temperature and age of the meat before cooking all played a role in turning the meat pink. We eliminated the problem by chilling the birds, which had been eviscerated, to less than 36 degrees within eight hours, using water in further processing that had been through a reverse

A circa 1985 photo of the main farm. There were still three fields of turkeys on range in this photo and the processing plant has had another three additions. Turkeys are now beginning to also be grown on satellite farms to decrease disease potential.

osmosis filter and cooking all the meat within five days of slaughter.

Another ongoing problem was toxins that occasionally appeared in corn used for turkey feed. These toxins had a detrimental effect on turkey growth. Looking at the corn gave no clue if toxins were present. Toxins were caused by excessive rainy weather on ripe corn before it was harvested. Excessive moisture in grain bins enabled toxins to multiply. Eventually, we secured test kits to test for the presence of four toxins. All incoming grain was tested. Corn that tested too high in toxins was rejected. If the test results were marginal it was fed only to the older turkeys.

Power outages were another challenge. Live turkeys needed a continuous supply of water and feed, and fans were necessary in some of the buildings to provide fresh air. The processing plant depended upon electricity for most of its operations. We had a tractor driven generator on each farm and a large diesel generator at the plant but when power went off, several people were required

to start all of the generators. Often when an automobile, with a drunk driver, hit an electric pole along the highway or a wind storm caused limbs to fall on power lines during the middle of the night we needed to start five to eight generators.

Amazing things were happening on the farm between 1985 and 1995. Of utmost importance was the employment of many outstanding new team members. Sherri Woods joined us in marketing, later becoming Mark's administrative assistant and is still working with him at Central New York Feeds. Joining us in 1987, was Joanne Nelson who served as office manager until 1998. Chip Hyde joined us in 1988 as farm manager and now is manager of Central New York Feeds. Other fine people who joined the business working with crops and growing turkeys, during this decade who were with us for at least 10 years were Bill Tack, Kevin Stahl, Don Bryant, Paul Kyle, Alan Peterson, Carl Horsford, Wally Kempinski, Josh Allen and John Manitta. Joining us in the processing plant for similar periods of time were Nick Basile, Lynn Hunter,

Carol Bennett, Linda Weinerth, Debbie Besaw, Luis Mercado, Rose Carvey, Mike Kreiger, Modesto Rivera and Luis Marrero. Sandy Bramble and Edna Parker took care of customers in the retail store while Rose Diefendorf and Rita Dewey worked in the office. Joan Reeves joined us in regulatory compliance and as the plant manager's administrative assistant, Iris Pero who had retired from a career in nutrition came to help in product development, Jason Kiteveles started in processing, later heading up warehousing and traffic, Fred Davis became responsible for plant maintenance and Hans Goodnow worked with him. The excellence of all of these people along with the ones previously employed was absolutely amazing.

Roxanne Parmele joined the business in 1989 as personnel manager in charge of human resources. Roxanne, while working for a human resource firm had helped us before coming full time. She brought our employee handbook up to date and increased needed discipline in human resources making sure we met all personnel regulatory compliance regulations and that each team member understood our policies.

Treating employees, whom we referred to as team members, as we would like to be treated had always been part of our family policy. It may have been partially because my dad and grandfather Bitz both had worked as hired men. Treating employees is not only morally right but when working with living things, it is critical to have happy and satisfied team members. In the case of Plainville Turkey Farm having satisfied team members was doubly important because we were striving for the best quality product we could produce and were charging a premium for it.

We printed our first monthly team member newsletter called Turkey Talk, in 1987. Later it was named, The Professor's Notes and finally, The Gobblers Gazzette. The name, Professor's Notes, was a reference to our animated turkey in the visitor center that was designed to be a source of knowledge concerning turkeys. Each month's newsletter was filled with information about the components of the business, sales, team members, recognitions, policies, jokes, sayings and minutes of the previous safety committee meeting. Each month it was eagerly anticipated by the team members.

A circa 1990 team member picnic with food, fun and games. Team members especially enjoyed throwing balls to dunk our several enterprise managers when each took his or her turn in the dunking booth.

We had many programs to make employment at the farm as safe and pleasant as possible. We also attempted, when appropriate, to reach beyond the farm to help ease team member's personal problems. We had a relationship with Child and Family Services, which offered counseling to team members who had domestic or financial challenges. Emergency loans of $50 were available with a no questions asked policy. One to three year loans, at cost, were also made to team members in amounts of from $300 to $2,500 for extenuating circumstances. A sunshine fund was established to provide cards or flowers for team members or their families in times of sickness, sadness or celebration. We also encouraged the team members to take adult education courses at local community colleges and paid them up to $500 a year for up to four years of study.

Each summer we had a farm family picnic for all team members and their families, catered at the farm, Syracuse Zoo or an area amusement center. Each year a number of retirees joined us at the picnic. There was always plenty of good food and games when it was held at the farm. This policy dated back to 1952, when there were only two employees besides Dad and myself. Team member and spouse were taken to a fine area restaurant each year, until 1975 when we changed to a picnic that included children. We also had Halloween dress up contests with prizes and a night at the Syracuse ballpark with free tickets. As the number of team members increased, vending machines were installed in the break rooms for those that wanted more than free coffee and cookies or wished to purchase lunch rather than bring it from home. By 1991, our expense for coffee and cookies reached $700 a month but it was a valuable policy we continued.

The safety of the team members, as well as the safety of the people they interacted with, was extremely important to us. Team members from each area of the farm's activities were elected by their fellow team members and met with either myself or Mark once a month. They brought suggestions and concerns from their fellow team members to the meeting. There was either an investigation or immediate action. The minutes of the meeting and any action taken were published in the next newsletter. Classes were provided for team members for certification in CPR and in first aid. In the 80s, we instituted a program requiring all prospective new team members to have a physical and be tested for drugs.

A number of positions in the processing plant required repetitive movements. Team members were urged to immediately tell their supervisor if they had pain so they could be given alternative work. We also installed a whirlpool to soothe elbows, arms, wrists and fingers if any team member was having problems.

An educational program was developed for the team members to better acquaint them with all of our policies, especially safety. Each year, team members were recognized and given prizes for years of work without a loss time injury. Many employees never received a loss time injury.

Many of the benefits that were provided for our team members dated back to the 50s and 60s. Each person received their birthday or alternate choice of day with pay. They were given three personal days to use whenever they were needed. Sick days with pay were also provided. If a team member didn't use their personal or sick days they could accumulate them and be paid for them upon reaching a maximum number of days. After being employed a year, each full-time team member earned two weeks of vacation with pay and after 10 years received three weeks each year. There was also a profit sharing plan dating back to the 50s, which evolved into a matching 401k program in the 1980s. We matched a team member's contribution to the plan up to a certain percentage of their wages.

Each year team members completing 5, 10, 15, 20, 25 and more years of service were recognized and given awards. We also had a "good idea" program with awards for the best idea each month. These ideas covered safety, efficiency and any suggestion that might improve some aspect of the operation. Cash prizes were awarded each month and one name was pulled from the monthly winners to receive a substantial cash prize each year.

For a number of years, the Baldwinsville Rotary Club held a yearly, Pride of Workmanship program. Almost every year we nominated one of our team members. Some of the winners were Janice Kline, Janice Schader, Nelson Bratt, Bill Rogers, Janice Congdon, Art Bratt, Linda Weinerth, Pat Castiglia, Char Cole, Paul Kyle, Modesto Rivera, Hans Goodnow and Nancy Gaul.

A few unusual team member related programs were a large pumpkin contest with prizes. We also gave a prize to the person that could guess the closest to the number of fresh turkeys we would sell each Thanksgiving. The Saturday before Thanksgiving, when everyone had been working, flat-out, for a week or more, we provided Kentucky Fried Chicken dinners for the employees during their lunch break.

As the number of team members increased we made additional efforts to interact with them. In 1991, we had reached 121 team members. When Mark became General Manager, he was available every Monday afternoon from 4:30 to 5:30 and encouraged team members to come to him with any problems, concerns or questions they might have. Another morale lifting gesture was when Roxanne Parmele, personnel manager, offered to spend a half-day working with any team member who invited her to join them. Every Monday, after we opened our new retail sales facility, five team members were invited to join Mark and I for lunch. Representatives from the plant, farm, feed mill and marketing were invited each week to encourage team members to get acquainted with each other. It was a time that each person could ask questions and make comments. It also gave Mark and I the opportunity to know each team member better.

Each week Mark had a lunch meeting with his management team where each manager shared what was happening, in their department, with the others. It also helped to avoid any problems or misunderstandings that might occur as one segment of the business interacted with the others. At each meeting, for several months, Stephen Covey's book, "Seven Habits of Highly Effective People" was discussed in depth. This program was helpful in developing a common understanding among the management team members of the appropriate actions expected of each person as they carried out their responsibilities.

In 1992, the farm offered six $1,000 scholarships to the graduates of the three surrounding central school districts. A scholarship was designated to go to one vocational student and one academic student at each school.

In May 1989, we opened a new free standing sales facility, with an attached visitor center, on the farm. Our small retail sales area in the dressing plant was inadequate and did not provide adequate parking or good visibility for customers to see oncoming highway traffic when entering and leaving. For me, the addition was a dream come true. We provided seating so customers could have a light lunch of several of our turkey products while there and even offered a 50 cent ice cream cone! We had a meat slicer for our cooked boneless products and provided meat trays for special occasions. The kitchen provided a facility to do some product testing as well as to prepare food for team members

Before we constructed the visitor center we had two turkeys, a pig and two goats for schoolchildren to see and pet.

Allen Bratt and June Allen are greeting the first guest at our visitor center, Fred Matthewson, in the early 1990s. Behind them is Farmer Pete on a Farmall F-20 tractor similar to the first tractor on the farm and Professor Plainville who was an authority on all things turkey. Farmer Pete and Professor Plainville chatted back and forth about turkeys and Plainville Turkey Farm.

Pens of farm animals in the visitor center. In addition to turkeys of different ages, there were sheep, goats, rabbits and a cow.

Round bales of straw and a little ingenuity can make interesting pumpkins and turkeys. This photo was taken on the lawn in front of the retail store and visitor center.

NY State Commissioner of Agriculture and Markets Dick McGuire speaking to the press the day we had an open house for our new retail store and visitor center.

and farm guests. We now had a place to educate potential wholesale customers as well as existing ones about the advantages of using Plainville turkey.

School children had been visiting the farm during all weather conditions for many years. We decided to build a barn next to the retail store to house a variety of farm animals for them to enjoy. To provide atmosphere, we mounted the old school bell from the Plainville country school next to the barn and rang it for each visiting class. A real silo was constructed between the retail store and visitor center that visitors had to walk through. The silo provided both a farm look on the outside and a farm

atmosphere on the inside. We had baby poults and full size turkeys along with miniature goats, lambs, rabbits and a pony in the visitor center. Later we had a cow, Buttercup, that had a calf. When Allen Bratt retired as a turkey grower he took care of the animals in the visitor center each morning and evening. Allen did a wonderful job and children were even able to see Allen milk the cow.

We purchased a Farmall F-20 tractor for the visitor center, similar to the first tractor that came to the farm in 1939. We also created an animated character named Farmer Pete to sit on the tractor. Farmer Pete and a large animated turkey named

Professor Plainville carried on a humorous educational conversation. Both characters were very popular with the children and other visitors.

A few years earlier, I had been to Australia and was enamored with the wallabies I had seen there. I heard of some available in Oregon, stopped by to look at them and had two shipped to the farm in 1992. They didn't fit in with our representation of local farming but visitors enjoyed seeing them. We only had them a couple of years because of disease complications but they were fun while they were there.

The retail staff kept a record of their visitors and in only the first few months that the retail store was open there were visitors from eight countries and 20 states. Agricultural leaders from around the world as well as school students and retail customers came to the farm. The retail store and visitor center weren't profit centers but were enjoyed by thousands of people including our team members and myself.

All parts of our farm operation were rapidly growing during this 10 year period. Chip Hyde arrived from Kentucky as farm manager in 1988, taking responsibility for crop operations and moving the mature turkeys to the processing plant. Later Chip became manager of the feed mill and is still doing an excellent job there.

Corn acreage continued to increase, and natural fertilizer from the turkeys was helping produce good yields. Traditionally, we had spread turkey manure on the fields as we removed it from the buildings or piled it in the fields for later spreading. Rain on the manure caused leaching of nutrients into the ground, losing much of its value, and eventually ending up in streams. To overcome this, we build a large building with a concrete floor to store manure until it was time to plant the crops. We developed a policy of spreading the manure and plowing it into the ground the same day it was spread, preserving its nutrients for the crops. We sold extra manure to a mushroom grower in Connecticut and to area farmers.

Our crop production was changing and in 1993, for the first time, we grew 30 acres of soybeans. We gradually increased their acreage to provide a rotation with corn, a practice beneficial to both crops. We bought more farms, constructed more

buildings and rented additional land to increase the land base and provide space for more turkeys.

As we had gradually increased the length of our turkey growing season, we continually grew more turkeys in buildings while the number grown on range remained constant. In the late 80s, wild birds transmitted bird flu to the turkeys on range and we had no choice but to discontinue growing turkeys outside. By growing our turkeys in buildings, we were able to keep wild birds away from them.

In the early 80s we discontinued using our mix mills to formulate feed and installed a vertical batch mixer to increase the uniformity of the feed, improve its palatability and decrease the amount of feed needed to grow a pound of turkey. After a few years we saw the need for additional improvement and more capacity was needed as well. In the early 80s, we had purchased property with two large grain bins and a railroad siding at Jordan, only eight miles away. We were unable to grow sufficient corn for our turkeys, and although we bought large quantities from neighboring farmers we needed corn from the midwest and used this facility to bring in corn.

In 1992, we decided to construct a feed mill on that site, which started operating in early 1993. Since the mill was constructed with substantially greater capacity than was needed for our turkeys we soon started making feed for some of the fine dairy farms that are numerous in Central New York. By 1995, we were producing several thousand ton of dairy feed each year along with about 20,000 tons of turkey feed. We increased the size of the delivery truck for our turkey feeds and arranged for independent contractors to deliver the dairy feed.

Turkey production was increasing each year, from 225,000 in 1985 to 447,000 in 1990. We were now buying all of our poults from the Goldsboro Milling Company in North Carolina with day old toms costing $1.52 and the hens $0.90 each.

In 1989, we made a significant change in our method of moving turkeys from the growing buildings to the processing plant. We designed and built variable-height flat trailers with hinged sides and with wire tops hinging upward. A load out shed was constructed on one corner of each growing building to allow us to drive the turkeys directly on to the trailers. At the processing plant the bed of the trailers were hydraulically adjusted to the dock

This photo shows a building with 16 test pens used to evaluate various feed ingredients. There were four replications for each ingredient tested. One was for the control, which was our present feed ration, and the other three were for potential changes. Growth and quality of finished product were both evaluated. These test pens were used for 20 years, evaluating over 50 possible changes, and provided valuable information needed to continually improve our turkeys.

height, and workers hung the live turkeys directly on the processing line. This removed almost all stress to the turkeys and made moving them much easier. Seldom were the turkeys on the trailers for more than a half-hour. It was a novel and successful idea that was unique to our operation. Driving the turkeys to the processing plant had been difficult during rainy weather or with snow on the ground. Trailers permitted us to grow turkeys on satellite farms, two or three miles away, and decrease danger of a potential disease moving among flocks.

About the same time we also created a rigid bio-security program to avoid the movement of any potential disease organism from one farm to another on team members or equipment. Special clothing was issued, foot baths installed and visitors prohibited without prior authority and special restrictions. In 1996, we installed showers on each farm and required the turkey growers to shower before entering their buildings and before leaving the farm that they were responsible for.

In 1990, we built 16 research pens for feed trials in one of our buildings. We used four pens for each of three feeds being tested, while reserving four pens for a control. These test pens were very successful. We tried many different feed formulations and learned information that was incorporated into the feed for all of our flocks. These test pens proved especially critical as Plainville Turkey Farm pioneered vegetarian diets, which required numerous unconventional ingredients and the use of various enzymes. We continued to use these pens for a variety of tests until the turkey business was sold in 2007.

We continually strived to improve conditions in the growing buildings for our turkeys and to improve the efficiency of the workers caring for the turkeys. Nipple waterers were installed in the brooding buildings to provide continuous fresh water for the birds. Truckloads of bulk shavings came to the farms, eliminating handling thousands of large bags of shavings. We used straw for litter in the growing buildings and changed from small

Four growing buildings and one brooding building on the Weller farm. 100,000 turkeys were grown in these buildings each year. They were herded onto large trailers and taken to the processing plant when they were ready to be marketed.

bales that were lifted several times by hand, before being spread, to large round bales that were lifted and moved by tractors and spread from a large tractor powered machine.

For many years the majority of our turkeys had been grown on our main farm where the processing plant was located. As numbers of turkeys increased, it became increasingly important to decentralize to diminish the threat of disease. In 1989, we purchased the Weller farm in Cayuga County and started construction of five large pole barns, which were completed in two years. This farm was isolated from our other farms and had capacity for 100,000 turkeys a year. Five years later, in 1994, we purchased the Stachurski farm and during the next two years built buildings designed for another 100,000 turkeys a year. In 1990, we approached Gary Somes to see if he would have an interest in brooding some poults for us, thinking it might fit well into his dairy operation. He felt that it would work well for both of us and two buildings were built on his farm. The poults were moved to our grow-out buildings at seven weeks of age. Gary and family did a fine job and a few years later both Gary and his son Pete became valuable full-time turkey growers at Plainville Turkey Farm.

Tragedy hit in May 1992 when a brooding stove in the building on the Manuel farm malfunctioned and started a fire. We lost 9,000 young turkeys and 124 feet of the building. There were 18,500 day old poults scheduled to arrive for that building

the following morning. Our team members and neighbors pitched in to move turkeys and prepare another building to house the poults, already on their way from North Carolina. The alternative building was ready when the poults arrived the next morning. I was extremely proud of Mark and all the crew who immediately took swift action to counter the potential crisis. Insurance adjustors were at the site the following morning and a contractor started rebuilding immediately. The replacement building was completed and housed poults five weeks later.

Marcus Henley joined us as processing plant manager in 1989. Marcus came from a large chicken processing operation in GA and brought a broad base of experience. The processing plant was the most labor intensive part of our operation, employing almost two-thirds of our team members.

We continually worked to improve working conditions and efficiency in the plant as the volume and variety of the products increased. For many years we had used tanks on wheels, filled with water and ice to cool our whole turkeys after evisceration.

We had at least 50 of these tanks and it was a big job moving them and keeping ice on them as it melted. We eliminated the tanks by installing a huge continuous chiller that held about 2,000 turkeys. The eviscerated turkeys went in one end and about two hours later came out the other end ready for boning or packaging as whole birds. There were several large compressors and a heat exchanger combined with air pumps to keep the water moving and rapidly cool the birds. We also had a large overhead ice machine that allowed us to add ice to aid in the cooling as needed.

Some years earlier had we moved away from the large bake ovens to roast turkey rolls and breasts in small roasting pans. We purchased a large oven, the size of a small room, that could be used for either smoking or cooking meat. Multiple large racks on wheels, with layers of shelves, holding as many as 60 whole birds each, were rolled into the oven. The appropriate programmed cycle was set and several hours later hundreds of turkeys, breasts or other cooked products were fully cooked. There was also a cycle to shower the products, in the bags they were cooked in, to partially cool the product before rolling the racks into large coolers. As volume increased we added additional ovens. We had an attachment for one of the ovens that burned hickory sawdust for smoking turkeys.

Throughout our years of operation, as technology made new equipment available we purchased this equipment to decrease labor costs and to improve the products we produced. We made numerous changes in the way we boned turkeys to improve efficiency. We changed from tables, to overhead moving lines, to round moving tables and to cones in efforts to improve. It was a challenge to find the method that was best for the worker, for the worker's efficiency and for the most complete removal of meat from the bones. After boning, a great deal of work was necessary in trimming the meat to remove pieces of fat, a bone particle or a small blood spot.

(above) Alice Warner in a circa 1990 photo of several racks of smoked turkeys that have just been removed from the smoker. Hickory wood chips were used for smoking.

(left) Four racks of boneless turkey breasts ready to be rolled into a large oven for cooking.

Hanging live turkeys on the processing line from our first trailer. Later the trailers were much larger and designed to move up and down to provide the correct height for both loading and unloading the turkeys.

Boning a turkey on a rotary moving line. The team member has several knives in her scabbard, along with a steel to have a sharp knife all the time. Note that she had a guard on her arm and hand to avoid injury.

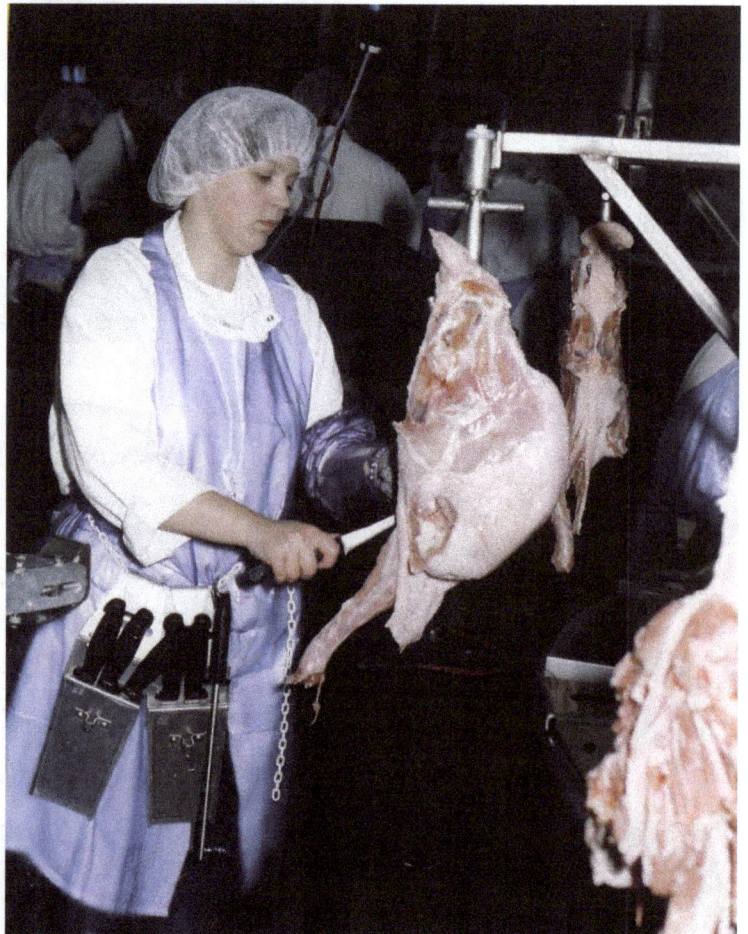

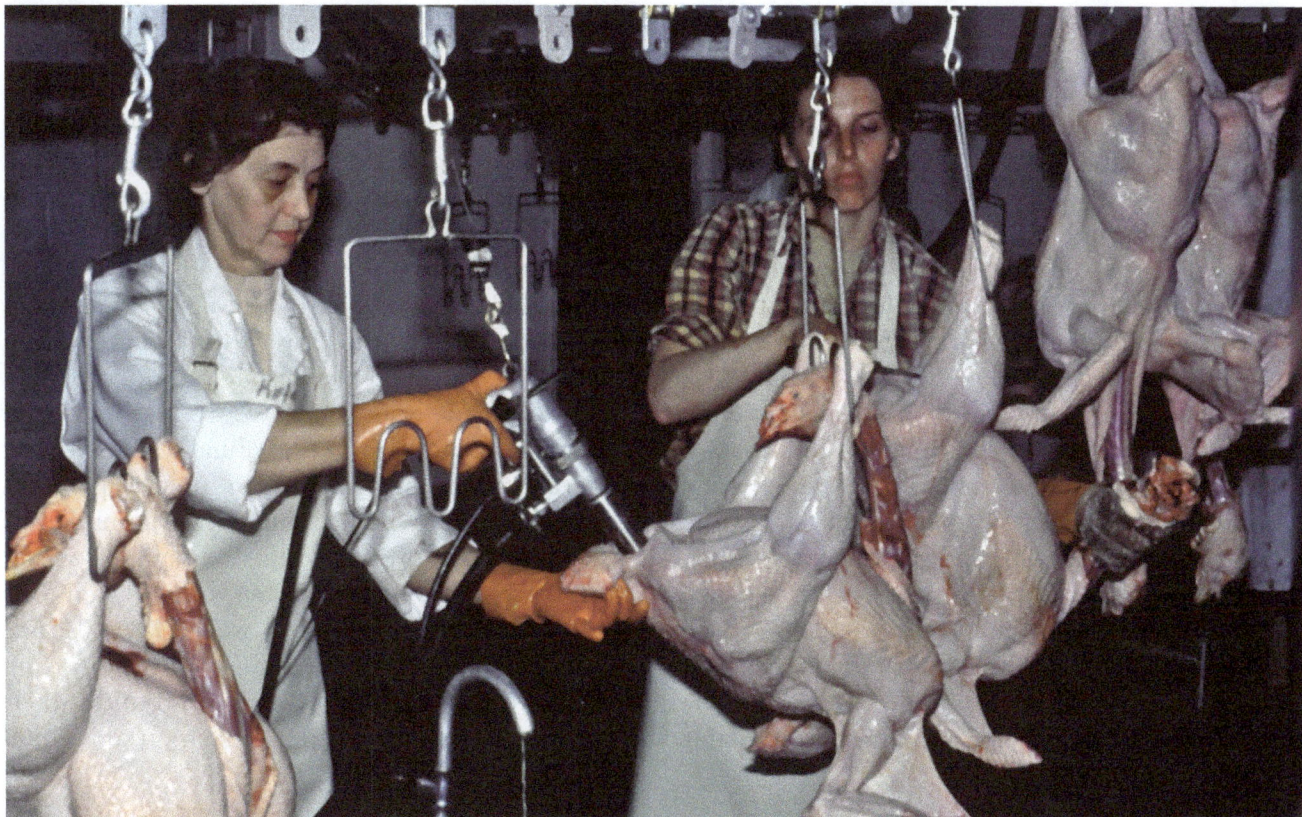

Kate Bennett is using a vacuum gun to remove the turkeys lungs and reproductive organs. Char Cole is changing the turkeys from three-point to two-point suspension in preparation for head and neck removal.

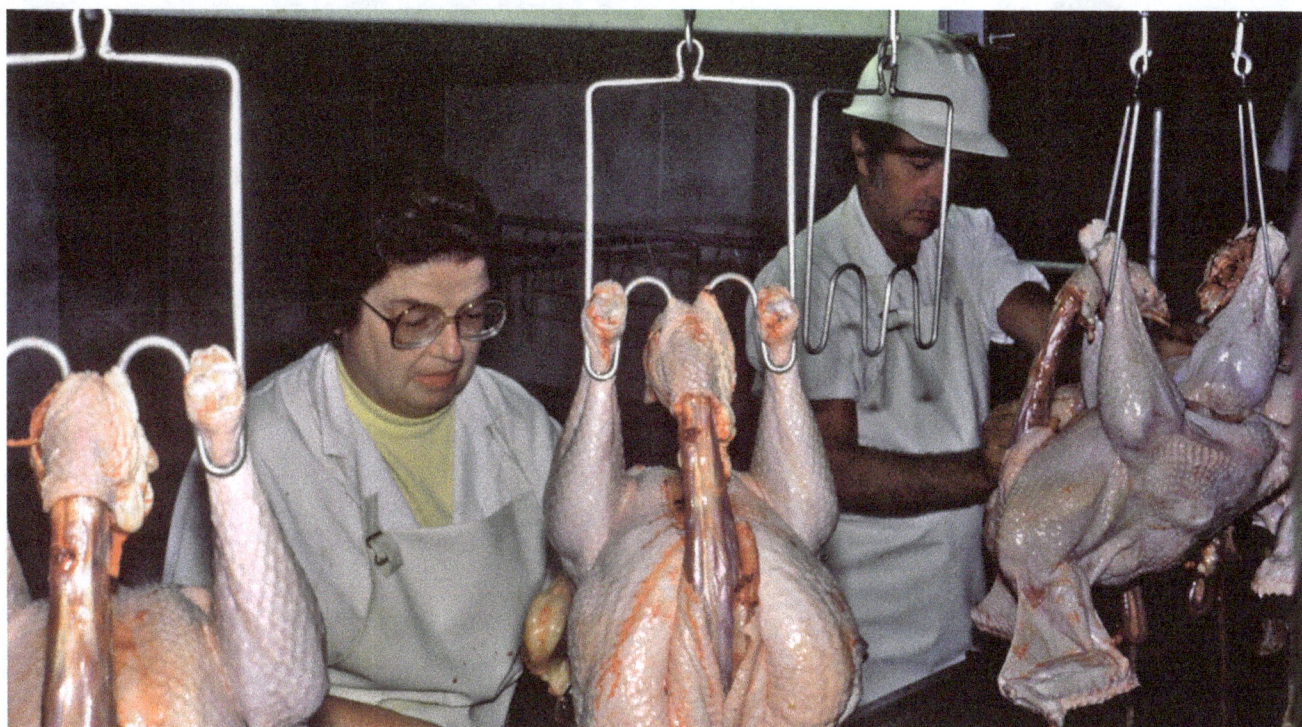

Janice Kline, a Plainville team member, is assisting USDA Inspector Robert Dingman by removing and destroying any part of a turkey that is damaged. When Plainville went under USDA Inspection to be able to ship their products out of New York, Inspector Dingman changed from New York State Inspection to the USDA Inspection Service.

We produced a high quality product and spent a great deal more time trimming meat than most of our competitors.

As far back as 1950, we had used electric stunning to lessen the trauma during the slaughter of the turkeys. First stunning was done by the person bleeding the turkey and later it was done automatically as birds moved on the line before bleeding. Stunning was a precise art to both remove trauma to the birds and improve their bleeding. We continually refined the process.

In 1985, Ron Ramstad joined us as marketing manager. Throughout the US small businesses were disappearing and being replaced by larger ones. Our traditional markets of small grocery stores and meat markets were being replaced by large supermarkets. Our small distributors were being replaced by larger ones. To stay in business we had to reach out further and obtain larger customers. Another challenge was that we had little control over the price of turkey other than through superior quality

and product differentiation. For example, in 1990 the wholesale price of turkeys was over 10% less than it had been the year before and about 20% less than in 1988. Our costs changed very little from year to year. Cycles of high and low prices continually encouraged many turkey producers to increase production when prices were favorable and later be forced out of business during periods of low prices.

We had supplied nearby universities including Syracuse, Cornell and Oswego with turkey for a number of years. Later we began to supply colleges scattered throughout the state. We also increased our business with large supermarkets including Federal Markets in the Buffalo area, Tops, P&C and Wegmans. We had attempted, for a number of years to get our products into Wegmans. Working with these large supermarkets often taxed our resources. During April 1991 we sold 3,000 cases of smoked breasts to Wegmans and during one week in July sold 32,000 pounds of ground turkey. That year we sold about 40,000 fresh turkeys, 2,600

Harry and Bob Bitz, with helpers, driving bronze toms to the processing plant in the late 60s. Turkeys are afraid of anything different, including the yellow line down the center of the road. Later we painted over the center line, where turkeys had to cross the road, to make driving them easier.

Almost every year we constructed one or more buildings. Mark Bitz has a transit to measure elevations as a site for a new building was graded.

cooked turkeys, 4,000 bone-in-raw-breasts, 60,000 pints of gravy and 20,000 pounds of dressing along with a variety of other items for Thanksgiving. We were a continually growing business!

In 1991, we received a great deal of publicity when a wire photo of our team members, driving a flock of turkeys across the road to the processing plant, was printed nationally. We also had Professor Plainville doing local radio commercials at this time. Periodically we invited our wholesale customers to the farm and our visitor center, to show them the operation and the many products we produced. SYSCO, a large institutional food supplier, and Roche Brothers stores in Boston became customers.

One of the first things Mark did, upon his return to the farm was to do a product costing and contribution report to compare both the cost and profit of each of our products to the rest of the turkey industry. He found that our costs were the highest, compared to our giant competitors. It became obvious that for Plainville to remain a viable business we needed to have significant product differentiation.

In the late 1980s, we produced the first "All Natural Ingredient Deli Line," free of added nitrates, phosphates, starches and gums. We were moving toward all natural products. In 1993, we introduced all natural dressing, gravy and cranberry sauce. Producing an excellent gravy without

modified food starch proved especially difficult. We also added safe handling instructions to all of our fresh products that year. A year later the farm was producing 10 different all natural products.

About this time Mark announced that our turkeys were going to be grown without the use of any antibiotics. It was standard practice in the poultry industry to feed low levels of antibiotics on a continuous basis to keep the birds healthy and increase their growth rate. I thought he was crazy to do this. We were growing several hundred thousand turkeys in confinement and it appeared to be a risky move. In 1993, we were approached by a Whole Foods buyer requesting us to grow turkeys without antibiotics. This undoubtedly helped Mark realize he was heading the business in the right direction.

We had always provided more space for our turkeys than was provided by the rest of the industry and Mark increased the amount of space even more. For several years we were building additional buildings to provide this extra space and not increasing the number of turkeys we grew. Amazingly, our birds lived and prospered. Looking back, the elimination of antibiotics, the additional space and changes we made in the turkeys' feed improved their growth. It was a needed change, for the benefit of humans, because the continual use of antibiotics in meat animals increases bacterial

The farm had very little level land so bulldozers were used to secure correct grades. We often allowed the building to slope with the land, a limited amount, to minimize the amount of earth that needed to be moved.

resistance to antibiotics, which decreases their effectiveness for humans. It was a move well ahead of the rest of the poultry industry that still has many large producers using antibiotics. To remove antibiotics successfully requires excellent care for live birds and good management practices.

A team composed of our in-house personnel was formed to develop, adapt and improve our turkey products. Not only were we instigating cutting-edge practices in growing our turkeys but we were also busy creating new products and changing existing products to better meet the needs of customers.

The printing on our package was our billboard and our means of communication with our customers. A team of five of our brightest people was created to work on our labels along with a graphic designer. Many hours of thought and work went into creating our differentiation and communicating it on our labels.

In 1995, Barb Quijano became sales and marketing manager. Barb had no experience marketing food products but could think outside of the box and quickly developed a marketing

program to differentiate Plainville turkeys and turkey products. A slogan, "Purely Delicious, Naturally Nutritious" was adopted, new graphics were designed for the delivery trucks and the farm was represented at numerous food shows. Our differentiation from other producers was significant in several ways that were important to consumers. Plainville turkeys were grown without antibiotics, raised without any animal byproducts, grown with animal friendly practices and with only the use of natural ingredients in our products.

Amazing and unheard of trendsetting innovations were occurring at Plainville Turkey Farm. Plainville was the first and only meat company to receive permission from the USDA to put, "Animal Friendly Practices" on its labels. After putting into place a number of unusual and expensive growing practices on our farms, it took two years to accomplish this feat, and included letters of testimony from several professionals. Plainville turkeys had always been at the 'top of the heap' but now was positioned far ahead of the competition.

SIX

1995 to 2012

All segments of the operation were growing during this period but none as rapidly as the five fold increase of corn and soybean production. Crop production increased from less than 1,000 acres in 1995 to about 5,000 acres in 2007. A combination of economy of scale, a large supply of natural organic fertilizer, a developing market for organic products and talented team members drove the increase.

Farms were purchased (Appleby, Bratt, Duger, Cox and Somes) and additional land was rented from area landowners. Large truck mounted manure spreaders, with flotation tires to permit spreading on soft ground, were purchased and an additional manure storage site was constructed on the Weller farm. A concrete pad of more than an acre was built on the Cox farm for composting manure and in 2003 an addition was added to the farm shop.

With the crop portion of the business increasing, Mark and Josh Allen formed the partnership, Central New York Crops. By 2007, they were growing many acres of organic corn and soybeans as well as traditional corn, soybeans and wheat. There was a strong market for organic grain and traditional grains were marketed at the feed mill.

Feed production at the Jordan feed mill was also increasing rapidly. Production tripled from about 18,000 tons of turkey feed and 4,000 ton of dairy feed in 1996 to 20,600 ton of turkey feed and 46,200 ton of dairy feed in 2005. Because of extra capacity at the feed mill, sales to dairy farms were encouraged.

In 1996, CNY Feeds exhibited at Empire Field Days and in 1998 provided an appreciation dinner for its customers at Plainville Farms Restaurant. Improvements were being made to the mill with additional feed bins and a large building built to store orange pulp, which was fed to dairy cattle.

New York State increased requirements for storage of fuel in 1998. This required us to build a new fuel depot to provide fuel for our many trucks and tractors. We also were required to replace the fuel oil tanks at the processing plant to comply with the new regulations.

Securing disease free poults and keeping them free of disease was always a challenge. During 1996 and 1997, Meleagris Gallopavo (MG) hit about half of our birds bringing substantial morbidity and increased mortality. Unfortunately it came from a hatchery on the baby poults, requiring us to change hatcheries. With turkey numbers increasing, it was especially important to prevent a problem on one farm traveling to another. Because of this disease, in 1996, we began a program of starting, growing and marketing all the birds on each individual farm before starting another batch of baby poults on that farm. Once the turkeys were marketed from a farm, we cleaned and disinfected the buildings, hopefully breaking any disease cycle.

Along with total farm turkey depopulation we provided the turkeys with an additional 30% space in the growing buildings and required team members to shower in and shower out, on each

The farm's feed mill on a Conrail siding at Jordan. Ingredients arrived by both trucks and railcars and finished feed was transported by tractor trailer to the turkey buildings as well as a number of dairy farms, which we supplied with feed.

A tractor trailer feed truck filling one of the bins next to a turkey building. We changed from a dump body that blew the feed with air into the bins to an auger on a tractor trailer for faster unloading, greater capacity and the elimination of separation of ingredients caused by blowing the feed.

The Stachurski farm had five growing buildings, a brooding building and a utility building. It was designed for about 120,000 turkeys a year. Attached to the barn, on the right side, is an addition where the trailers were backed in and where the turkeys were herded onto the trailers. In the middle foreground are several pallets of pine shavings, which were used for litter in the buildings.

This turkey growing building on the Duger farm constructed in 2006 and was the last growing building we constructed prior to selling the turkey business.

farm. Providing 30% more space, required us to construct 30% more barns to maintain the same level of production.

We formed a committee of our most savvy team members to help us through this difficult period. By consistently working to overcome our problems they were able to change adversity into a marketing advantage and make our labels a billboard that promoted our animal friendly practices.

The changes we made gradually improved the livability and growth of our turkeys. By 2003, we had 95% livability of our toms and 97% livability with our hens. This was much better than the rest of the industry and we were growing our turkeys without any antibiotics!

Expansion of turkey growing buildings continued with a large building constructed on the Duger farm. Gary Somes also added another

brooding building on his farm. Josh and Fred Allen constructed a large growing building on their farm in 2002, and added two more later. We didn't have the resources, however to grow all the turkeys we needed on our farms so reached out to growers in other areas of the country.

In 2002, we contracted with two Minnesota farms to grow 95,000 toms for us. The growers did a good job but because the Minnesota processing plant did a poor job eviscerating the turkeys, two years later we discontinued our agreement with the growers.

In 1996, the USDA approved 26 new labels that we had requested, a major feat in itself. An empty meat plant in Liverpool, previously owned by Swift Meat Co., was purchased, remodeled and put into operation in 1998. Our Plainville plant was bursting at the seams and this expansion permitted

The Plainville turkey cooking plant at Liverpool. Many turkey products including whole turkeys were cooked in this facility and then shipped all over the country. Before we purchased the property it had been a Swift & Co. meat plant. Cooking on this site removed the cooked products from proximity to our live turkeys, which helped to ensure a safer product.

cooking, smoking and roasting of turkey at a separate facility. This was also a positive move to help avoid a potential transfer of bacteria from live birds to cooked product.

In 1998, the USDA announced that on January 1, 1999 a program called Hazard Analysis Critical Control Points (HACCP) was to go into effect in all meat and poultry processing plants. We made the required physical changes and established the necessary procedures to successfully become part of the program. The program was designed to eliminate possible hazardous food situations before they could start. It required many, many hours of labor by our staff to accomplish this.

The processing plant was a busy place and changes were being made there. In 2000, Josh Allen, who had been working mostly with crops, turkey growing and machinery repair, replaced Marcus Henley as processing plant manager. Bella Stahl, who had been working on special projects including HACCP, became manager of the Liverpool plant. Both Josh and Bella were highly talented and performed very well.

For Thanksgiving in 2000, we processed 85,000 fresh turkeys, a new record. We received

a big surprise, however, about a week before Thanksgiving, during our busiest time of the year. The US Department of Immigration raided the plant and removed 16 of our fine workers. When we hired these workers we checked their green cards, but found out after the raid, that all 16 had been forgeries. The other employees pitched in to fill the gap, working additional overtime.

For several years, to help meet the demand for our products, we had purchased boneless turkey meat and thawed it in circulating water. In 2001, we bought and installed a meat thawing oven that held 6,720 pounds per batch. The oven maintained the temperature a few degrees above freezing, while rapidly moving air safely and conveniently thawed the meat.

By 2002, our Thanksgiving production had reached 100,000 fresh turkeys, 13,000 cooked and smoked turkeys and 14,000 bone in raw breasts in addition to a multitude of other turkey products. Demand was rapidly increasing.

Ground turkey and other product sales were also increasing. This required the purchase of a large carbon dioxide tank to help keep our products cool during processing. Carbon dioxide, as it

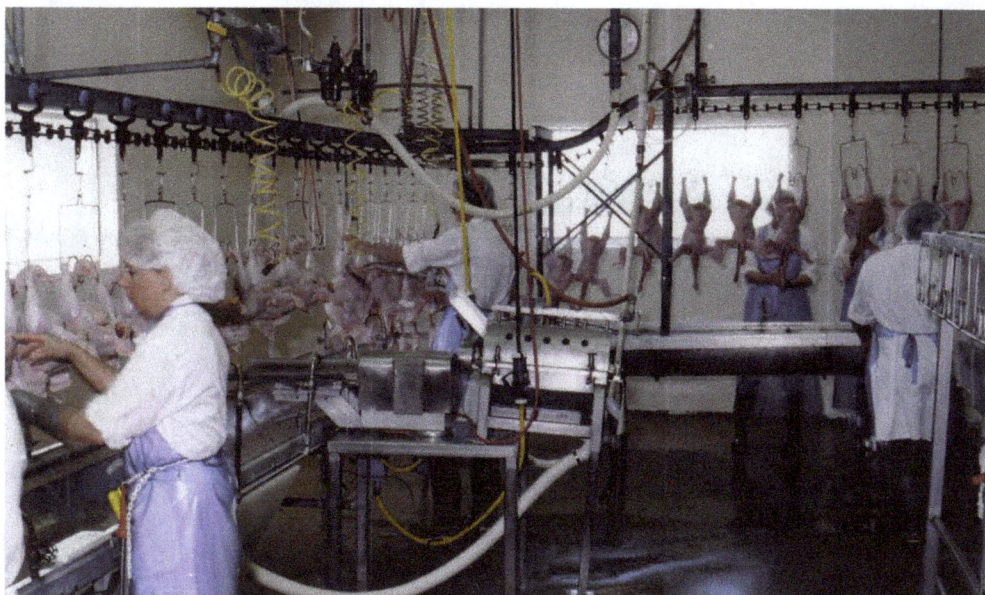

Turkeys being eviscerated before going to the chiller for cooling. About 13 birds a minute were processed with the mechanized equipment available.

evaporated, maintained a safe temperature in the meat and wasn't detrimental to the products being produced. We also installed a tray packaging line to produce 30,000 trays of turkey products a week.

10,000 to 12,000 live turkeys were being processed each week along with 3,000 purchased canner pack turkeys (eviscerated turkeys packaged in bulk for further processing) and also bought frozen boneless skinless meat. By 2004, we were receiving 225,000 canner packs, grown for us in Canada.

In 2005, Josh Allen became General Manager and we employed a new processing plant manager. Josh continued to oversee the processing plant operations but was also able to become more involved with the other aspects of farm operations that he had always enjoyed.

The following year, New York State decreed that we must provide both secondary and tertiary treatment for wastewater from our processing plant. This required the investment of more than 1.2 million dollars and consumed about seven acres of prime farmland. For many years our wastewater had been flowing into a natural lagoon with good clean water coming out the other end. Increasing government control and regulations were costing more and more each year and taking a larger share of each managers' time.

In 2006, we made two more additions to our main processing plant and purchased a meat boning machine for wings and drumsticks. It saved a great deal of hand labor and helped provide more meat for ground turkey.

The Liverpool plant was operating very well under Bella's guidance and with the help of several long term excellent team members. It had the honor of receiving the Onondaga County waste water award for excellence in 2007.

With the distinct differentiation of Plainville turkeys from its competitors including the removal

Plainville's smoked boneless breast, roast boneless breast, turkey ham and turkey pastrami ready for customers to enjoy.

75

A flock of day old poults in one of our modern brooding buildings equipped with automatic waters and feeders, and with controlled ventilation.

Large strutting turkey toms ready for market. When reaching sexual maturity the toms become quite aggressive and spread out their feathers to impress any hen turkey that might be in the area. New team members who have never been in a building full of mature toms are quite intimidated as the toms chase them while they do their work in the building.

A Plainville roast turkey ready-to eat. It took a great deal of both knowledge and effort to produce Plainville turkeys for the discriminating public.

of antibiotics, use of animal friendly practices and grown without animal byproducts, we were able to move from market pricing to 'cost plus' for our products. A change like this cannot be successful without publicity and it required added emphasis on promotion and marketing. We had a variety of exhibits at the New York State Fair and were featured on TV Food Network. Plainville also exhibited its products at the Washington Dairy-Deli Show to exhibitors and buyers from all over the US. New labels carried the phrases Nature's Way, Veggie Grown and Heart Lite. A fresh whole Plainville turkey, against broad competition, received a national taste award. The feed and care provided our turkeys not only made them taste excellent but chemical tests also clearly proved the differences with laboratory analysis.

In 2002, growth was fueled to a large extent through the use of our products by Whole Foods. Other new customers were Giant Foods, Ukrops and D'Agostino's, totaling over 300 additional stores.

Most of these stores carried one or two of our products rather than the full line. A customer appreciation dinner was held at our Cicero Restaurant, with over 100 attending and with a Syracuse University Professor as the main speaker. Sadly many of our long time customers were closing their doors, including Peter's Markets and Sweetheart Market due to competition from large chain stores.

Product improvement continued, including the addition of caramelized vegetables to our turkey gravy and the production of half-turkeys for smaller families. The gravy not only was excellent but was low in fat and healthy. I didn't feel there would be much of a market for half-turkeys but surprisingly they proved to be well accepted.

Our retail store and visitor center proved popular with 30,000 people visiting the farm in 1996, 6,000 of them school children. We developed a video of the farm to show visitors how the turkeys were grown and processed. In the fall we sponsored a harvest celebration weekend with extra activities.

In 1997, we constructed a 54 by 90 foot building, next to the retail store and visitor center, called The Pioneer Experience. For several years I had been collecting farm related antiques of the 1800s, that were in common use as Upstate New York was settled and developed. The centerpiece of the building was an authentic log cabin similar to

The farm retail store is in the center and the visitor center is the building on the left beyond the silo. The Pioneer Experience is the building on the right. In 2003, the retail store was closed and became the corporate offices. The visitor center then was also closed and used for team member meetings.

77

This building was constructed in 1997 to house the Pioneer Experience. On each side of the door in the center of the building are a pair of old millstones.

An authentic replica of an early log cabin that we had constructed for the Pioneer Experience. It had a mud and stick fireplace and chimney, along with authentic furnishings inside the cabin.

This shows some of the farm antiques in the visitor center. The large red object in the corner is a grain reaper and there is a mowing machine, also from the 19th century in front of it. A wooden dump rake hangs on the ceiling and an early straw horse collar hangs on the left.

Some antique household items in the Pioneer Experience. A pie safe is on the left with a basket for goose feathers and a cheese box on top. A birthing chair sits next to it and on its right is an early country table and a corner cupboard.

many that had been constructed during the early years of settlement. There was also a large room for group presentations as well as a television for a video presentation about early pioneer life. We had a number of visitors, but like most museums there was never an overflow crowd. When Mark closed the retail store and visitor center in 2003, I decided to have an auction of the larger antiques and moved many of the smaller ones to my garage.

Sales of our turkeys and turkey products were increasing about 20% annually and reaching into distant parts of the country. The retail store and visitor center were bringing many people to the farm, which had both positive and negative aspects. Our retail sales had become a smaller portion of our business and with many people coming to the farm, the potential of disease increased. Our products were readily available in many stores including our Cicero restaurant. Because of these factors and $30,000 in losses from it each year, Mark decided to close the visitor center and retail store. Many customers, who had come to the farm to buy their turkey for several generations, were especially disappointed but closing was a wise business decision.

In 2006, Price Chopper and Wild Oats became two of our larger customers and offered Plainville's products in many new communities. The same year we were honored to be selected by the New York State Agricultural Society as New York's agricultural business of the year.

The following year we bought a 10 acre site with a 66,000 square foot building at Interstate Island, near the junction of the New York State Thruway and Route 690. We had rented additional freezer and refrigerated space for a number of years. This building provided an excellent location and sufficient room for our needs. A large freezer and a large cooler were constructed in the building and a number of dock spaces were added for loading and unloading tractor trailers. Our maintenance people did most of the work, including removing over 1,200 ten-wheeler truck loads of dirt from the site.

People are key to a successful business and Plainville had many exceptional people. Earlier chapters mentioned long term team members who were at Plainville more than 10 years who had arrived by 1985. Fine people continued to join the business. Receiving awards in 2006 for working approximately 10 years were Roberto Jimenez, Hilario Ortiz, Luis Torres, Jeff Smith, Ed Harrison, Tom VanHorn, Will Hamlin, Becky Hendricks, Jeremy Gould, Angela Hernandez, and Jerry Crego. At the same award ceremony, nine team members received awards for 20 years of service. Not mentioned at that ceremony were most of those, working between 10 and 20 years as well as a number over 20 and some even more than 30 years.

This is a building located near the intersection of the Thruway and Rt. 690 that was purchased and remodeled in 2006 for use as a freezer, cooler and marketing offices.

Beginning in 2001, Plainville began to give an award to team members that had provided exceptional service to the business. I was honored when it was named, the R.W. Bitz Master's Award. Team members honored were given a week extra vacation, $1,500 for a trip and $300 spending money. Some of the team members honored during the following years were Char Cole, Janice Shader, Bill Rogers, Bill Tack, Luis Torres, Mike Krieger, Kevin Stahl, Jason Kiteveles, Modesto Rivera, Nelson Bratt, Hans Goodnow, Pat Castiglia and Sherri Woods.

A variety of new team member contests and awards occurred during this period. There was an exercise challenge extending for a month at a time where teams of four, chosen by those wishing to participate, established a goal. The goal might be as simple as walking 30 minutes, three times a week or two 20 minute basketball games. The ones completing their goals received a worthwhile prize. There was also a holiday weight challenge with cash prizes, designed to help prevent team members from putting on additional weight over the Christmas holidays. There was a pumpkin decorating contest in the fall and a dental reimbursement program instituted. In 1997, 54 team members won attendance awards and in 2004 the number increased to 74. The period covered for the attendance awards was a full year, in an attempt to encourage regular attendance. The majority of our team members worked in the processing plant. Some who didn't enjoy their work were not always regular in their attendance and didn't complete a full year.

An office is an essential and busy part of any thriving business. In 1998, Tim Gaul joined us as

This is a circa 1992 photo similar to Norman Rockwell's famous painting "Freedom from Want." Bob and Janice Bitz are presenting the roast turkey to some of Plainville's team members who are sitting around the table in the same manner as Rockwell's subjects.

information systems manager. The following year he set up a new and improved accounting system.

After we closed the retail store and visitor center in 2003, the store was converted into corporate offices. The kitchen continued to be used to prepare meals for team member special meetings and to prepare Plainville products for prospective customers to taste. It also provided an ideal location for interaction with our wholesale customers.

The visitor center became a meeting space for team member training and team member meetings.

In 2007, we interacted with our growers in Ohio and Canada for Animal Humane certification, which was recognized at our Plainville location. We attempted to be considerate of our turkeys and wanted our other growers to follow similar practices.

In August 2007 Mark sold the turkey operation, including 600 acres of land with buildings, to Hain Pure Protein Corporation, which was a joint venture between Hain-Celestial Group, Inc. and Pegasus Capital Advisors, L.P. Mark had become increasingly disillusioned with the cost of doing business in New York State. Rather than being a friend of businesses working to create jobs, it seemed like the State was more often an adversary of business. Mark thought that Hains' resources would grow the business and continue our tradition of producing high quality products. He agreed to advise them for a year.

Loading rectangular bales of straw, each weighing over 1,000 pounds, on a tractor trailer.

This is a grain drill that plants seeds without any previous tillage, reducing erosion and decreasing the use of fuel and extra traveling over the ground, to plant a crop.

Organic fertilizer (manure) is being loaded on a spreader truck to be spread on the land for growing corn. The manure was stored under cover and immediately plowed into the ground after it was spread.

One of a half dozen live turkey trailers that were used to bring turkeys from the growing buildings to the processing plant. The turkeys walked onto the trailers and when they reached the processing plant were hung on a moving processing line.

A large combine with a 30 foot grain head unloading soybeans into a transfer cart. The transfer cart carries the soybeans to the tractor trailers near the main highway, which is especially important if the ground is wet.

A conventional 12 row corn planter planting corn on ground that has been plowed and fitted for a seedbed.

SEVEN

Plainville Farms Restaurants

The success of McDonald's, Burger King and other fast food chain restaurants during the 60s and 70s made me wonder, "Why not turkey?" I was a strong believer in obtaining as much of the consumer's food dollar as possible, so providing the customer with a knife, fork and a plate filled with fine food seemed a logical choice.

Since I knew almost nothing about the restaurant business, other then selling turkey to restaurants, some expertise was needed. Victor Johnson, who a few years earlier had worked part-time for me selling turkey rolls, operated a successful fast food restaurant near Skaneateles. We talked about the possibility of opening a fast food restaurant featuring Plainville turkey and both felt it could be a successful venture.

It seemed wise to obtain an opinion from a knowledgable disinterested party so I contacted Stan Warren, a Cornell Agricultural Economics Professor of whom I had a great deal of respect. We met with Stan and Max Brunk, an Agricultural Economics Professor in Marketing. Vic and I explained what we intended to do and after asking us some questions they recommended that we forget about the idea of opening a turkey restaurant. They felt that turkey was too specialized, and since neither of us were intending to be an active on-site partner, success would be unlikely. In other words, starting a turkey restaurant would not be a good decision.

Subsequently we ignored their advice and started searching for an appropriate site to build a restaurant. Since we had a limited budget some of the sites we looked at were out of our price range. We found a five acre site on Route 11, just north of Cicero that had been part of the Pardee farm, which was split by Interstate 81. The Pardee family were willing to hold a mortgage on the property and Vic and I were able to finance the restaurant through Merchants National Bank and Trust Company. We were on our way toward a turkey restaurant!

Jumping ahead 25 years in time, I stopped at the busy Cicero restaurant for dinner one day and sitting at a table were Professor Max Brunk and his wife enjoying a turkey dinner. We exchanged pleasantries and then Max turned to me and said, "Bob, it looks like I gave you some poor advice 25 years ago!"

There was an old silo standing next to a barnyard where we were planning to build the restaurant. We rented a bulldozer, buried the silo and used our farm trucks to draw many loads of gravel to cover the old barnyard and prepare a site for the building. Vic and I drew the gravel and prepared the site in our spare time.

We started construction of the building in the spring of 1973 and had the restaurant completed for opening in August. I acted as general contractor and hired a variety of subcontractors for construction, plumbing, heating, refrigeration, electrical and equipment. We were fortunate to have good subcontractors who worked well together and the building was completed in a timely manner and at a reasonable cost.

We had a large mural on one of the restaurant walls depicting the first Thanksgiving dinner held

Plainville Farms Restaurant coming into being in 1973. Bruce and Mark Bitz are standing by the two posts that will hold the sign for the restaurant.

The site for the Plainville Farms Restaurant was originally part of the Pardee farm that had previously been cut into two parcels by Rt. 81. There had originally been a dairy barn and silo on the site.

A photo of Plainville Farms Restaurant shortly after it opened. Note the pen of live turkeys in front that were there for a few months. We soon realized that they were tempting to vandals and removed them.

by the Pilgrims and the Indians. Barbara Enders, an artist friend did the painting. My wife, Janice, and I met Barb at the restaurant one evening and used a slide projector to show appropriate images on the wall. We then made rough outlines of the key components of the mural on the wall. The following day Barb returned and completed the mural that has been enjoyed by thousands of people in the succeeding years.

Although it was to be a fast food restaurant we tried to bring a bit of the farm to it. I had my 14 year old son, Mark, build attractive natural wood containers to house the garbage cans and make wooden pegs where customers could hang their coats. My wife Janice, put a great deal of effort into selecting appropriate wall paper, paint and decorations for the restaurant. We built a small pen in front of the restaurant to hold a few live turkeys. A great deal of planning and effort had gone into the restaurant and we were proud of our accomplishment.

Although I have seldom had a physical problem, the day before the grand- opening of the restaurant, while playing tennis with my daughter, I popped a tendon in my leg and attended the grand opening on crutches. Vic hired the necessary employees and served as general manager. We used our turkey rolls, served the customers on paper plates and they picked up their food at the counter, typical fast food.

August was an appropriate time to open a turkey restaurant. It gave the staff some time to become acclimated before the busy fall season when people think 'turkey'.

We had the normal challenges of starting a new business but things moved along quite well during the fall. Thanksgiving was a busy time with about 1,000 fresh turkeys sold and a good number of diners in the restaurant.

We knew that business would slack off after Thanksgiving but were shocked at how much it decreased. The winter of 1974 was a long slow time at Plainville Farms Restaurant! We were also learning some things. Customers didn't want to eat turkey from turkey rolls but wanted their turkey from the whole bird. Neither did they want to eat turkey from paper plates with plastic silverware. They also wanted their food brought to their table! To sum it up, our customers didn't want a fast food

turkey restaurant but wanted a traditional style restaurant.

We slowly changed to china plates and stainless steel cutlery. We started using whole turkeys and serving food at the tables. In the spring and into the summer business gradually improved and the red ink stopped flowing. Our dream of a fast food turkey restaurant was shattered! To survive we had to revert to the traditional restaurant approach, differing only that we featured turkey. We soon started offering fresh haddock dinners on Friday to complement the turkey.

Soon we offered a turkey buffet on Sunday, which proved to be a success and gradually extended the buffet to all day everyday. It became very popular. In 1979, the all you can eat buffet was priced at $4.95 , which included dessert and the turkey dinner cost $3.95. Red ink continued to flow every year from January to April but business increased sufficiently during the other months to make up for it.

Vic had his restaurant to operate and I was busy at the farm, so it was necessary to hire a manager. After we had been open a few years John Benedict, who had previously operated his own restaurant came as manager and served in that capacity for many years. John's wife, Sue and their three children also worked at the restaurant at various times along with John's brother and sister-in-law.

John brought stability to the restaurant and business prospered. The old Curry cafeteria became available at the corner of Erie Blvd. and James St. in Syracuse, one of the highest traffic locations in the Syracuse area. Vic and John were both in favor so I bought it in 1980 and remodeled it similar to our Cicero restaurant. John had a friend who had previously managed Burger King restaurants who was hired as manager.

Business didn't meet our expectations so we tried various promotions to improve it. We installed a large rotisserie to roast the turkeys and offered a six-minute lunch. If the customer didn't receive their meal within six minutes, it was free.

The Syracuse *Post Standard* provided weekly restaurant reviews and in 1983, when both of our restaurants were operating, they published a poor review of Plainville Farms restaurants. The review eventually provided a positive effect because many of our regular customers were upset with the review and wrote letters to the editor saying so. Two years later I decided to close the Erie Blvd. restaurant because it was not sufficiently profitable.

Vic and I had always had a fine relationship but in the 80s decided to terminate the partnership. He had other interests and offered to sell his half and I accepted his offer.

Still harboring a dream of success in fast food turkey, I opened a fast food turkey restaurant in the new Great Northern Mall on Rt. 31 in Clay. Tim Lang, who earlier had worked at a Friendly's restaurant was its manager. Initially it was a busy mall but the subsequent opening of the Carousel Mall diminished its business. Some years later we divided our space with part of it called the Fish Nook.

In 1990, we opened another Plainville's Turkey and More at the Fayetteville Mall. There was less customer traffic in the Fayetteville Mall and the restaurant didn't have sufficient volume to be profitable. In about 2000, we left Fayetteville due to significant changes taking place in the mall. A few years later we also decided to close Plainville's Turkey and More at the Great Northern Mall and Tim Lang became manager of the Cicero restaurant.

Early one spring Sunday morning in 1991 I received a phone call from John Benedict telling me that our Cicero restaurant had been vandalized during the night. Animal rights activists had spray painted all sides of our restaurant with graffiti, broken windows and even put glue in the locks. The restaurant looked terrible! The staff immediately went to work putting things into reasonable order and managed to open for business. The building looked very bad until we had it painted a few days later. It made headlines in the paper and

upset most of the people in the area. It was vandalized because we offered meat to our customers. Something the vandals didn't realize was that we provided better conditions for our turkeys than the rest of the industry.

A few months later, a meeting was organized at the Liverpool Public Library for animal rights activists and meat industry representatives to meet and exchange thoughts. I was the only person from the meat industry that went. I found it was impossible to make the activists understand that we cared about our turkeys.

In 1997, we did an extensive remodeling and addition to the Cicero restaurant. We installed a bakery, a large waiting room, an area of hydroponics, changed the buffet and extended the parking lot. We grew lettuce in the hydroponic area and served it on the harvest table. It was too small an area to produce a large quantity but customers enjoyed seeing it. We made bread, pies and cookies in the bakery and they were real popular.

For many years, almost from the time the Cicero restaurant opened, we provided customers with comment cards to fill out. We received many fine suggestions and comments by doing this. Since there was also a place for the server's name, the cards also helped to encourage good service. We were often amazed at the distant points that customers came from, even from Canada or PA for the sole purpose of eating at our restaurant. One time a writer from the *Post Standard* interviewed one of our patrons and then headlined a newspaper article, "They drove 300 miles for a meal."

The choice of the Cicero restaurant location was a stroke of luck. There were other sites we

Two bronze turkeys from our farm prepared by a taxidermist. They sat in a display case in the restaurant for many years.

The fireplace in the second dining room. Bob Bitz picked up the stones from the fields on his farm for a mason to use to build the fireplace.

would have chosen that were not affordable. The restaurant became a meeting place for travelers, a stopping point on long distance travel and the first stop for someone flying into the Syracuse Airport. Even though I asked my wife to count the cars passing by on Rt. 81, one of the times I examined the site before purchasing it, it was a lucky location. One of my dad's comments when we first opened the restaurant was, "I'm afraid its a little too far out in the country."

In the year 2000, we added two additional dining rooms to the restaurant that increased the seating capacity to about 300. Thanksgiving Day that year we seated 1,900 customers and had 200 additional take-out dinners. For that one day we served 77 thirty pound turkeys, 200 pounds of turkey ham, 750 pounds of dressing, 900 pounds of potatoes, 70 gallons of gravy, 300 pounds of squash, 350 pounds of corn, 250 pounds of mixed vegetables, 288 dozen rolls, 186 apple and 149 pumpkin pies. It was amazing the food that was consumed that day. The majority of the customers ordered the all-you-wish-to-eat buffet and left the restaurant well filled.

That year there was a program to decorate the Syracuse area with artificial life sized horses, each

painted and designed in a unique way. Sharon Bumann, a well known sculptor in the area, crafted a turkey-like cowboy on the back of a bucking horse that we placed in front of our Cicero restaurant. It was a masterpiece and enjoyed by the thousands of people who came to the restaurant.

Our business peaked at the restaurant before the dot-com bubble burst. We continued to have an excellent business but it eased off a bit with the recession.

In 1997, the CNY Sports Centre was being built between State Fair Blvd. and Rt. 690 south of Baldwinsville. The owners, wanted a fast food restaurant in the Centre that served healthy food, and invited us to start one similar to the one we had at the Great Northern Mall. We agreed to cooperate with them and operated it for five years, with Linda Sewruk serving as the manager.

Never learning to leave well-enough-alone, as soon as we closed our restaurant at the CNY Sports Centre, I purchased the former Top of the Hill Restaurant on old Rt. 5 west of Syracuse. Little had been done to the restaurant for a number of years so we did extensive remodeling before opening it in August 2002. Tim Lang served as general manager of both the Cicero and Camillus restaurants.

Bob Bitz and Sharon BuMann next to her creation of All-American Turkey at Plainville Farms Restaurant.

We bought a talking horse we named Hank, to interact with customers as they arrived and left the restaurant. Actually, it was only the head of a horse but we designed it so he appeared to be looking out from his stall in a barn. Children often looked behind the wall, in an adjoining dining room, to see if it was a real horse. My good friend, Jim Buswell, who has a great sense of humor, sometimes used a hidden microphone and as Jim talked Hank's lips move as if Hank was actually talking to the customer. It made great fun!

The business philosophy at our restaurants had always been good food at a reasonable price. We kept the price of our meals so they were affordable to most people. The Camillus restaurant provided seating for over 200 people and although we had many customers there were not enough to cover the overhead and make a fair return. After trying a number of promotions, about five years later, I decided to close the restaurant.

Restaurants are labor intensive and over the years, hundreds of people worked for us, serving fine food to our customers. For many young men and women, it was the first place they were ever employed. Many went on to college and had successful careers. For others, it was a fill-in job until a better opportunity came along. There were a number who worked over 20 years, making it a career. Totally different from

The restaurant, after several expansions, with the All-American Turkey in front.

the farm, where I rubbed shoulders with employees for many years, I had little interaction with our restaurant team members.

In 2005, at the age of 75, I decided it was time to retire from the restaurant business. My son, Mark, decided he would like to have the Cicero restaurant continue, first leasing it from me and later buying it. The operation continued until after Plainville Turkey Farm had been sold to Hains. When Mark owned Plainville Turkey Farm our turkeys had been free of salmonella. Unfortunately, salmonella entered the turkeys that Hain was growing.

Although it was beyond the control of Hain, salmonella bacteria came with each turkey delivered to the restaurant. Every possible precaution was taken at the restaurant but some customers reported they were made sick by eating at the restaurant. Mark closed the restaurant for a few days, did a thorough cleaning and then reopened.

He vowed to close the restaurant if any customers became sick again. Fresh turkeys were critical to the business and the restaurant would not succeed without them. A couple of months later, in January 2010, some more people became sick, the doors were closed and Plainville restaurants became part of the past.

The restaurant business was an interesting side-career for me. Would I do it again if I had my life to live over? Certainly, but I would have made a number of different decisions. The restaurants actually helped spread the fame of Plainville turkeys, especially with the Cicero restaurant's proximity to Rt. 81. Many customers had no idea that the farm was 20 miles to the west. The restaurants provided jobs for hundreds of people and eating enjoyment for thousands. All things considered my venture into restaurants was worthwhile!

Sandwiches
(On your choice of bread)

Roast Turkey Breast 2.50			**Fresh Ground Turkey** 1.75	
Delicious Plainville breast meat.			Fresh ground turkey—it's great!	
Smoked Turkey Breast 2.50			**Italian Style Turkey Sausage** . . 2.00	
Natural hickory smoked breast meat.			You won't believe it's turkey!	
Turkey Ham 2.00			**Ground Beef** 2.00	
It puts the pig to shame.			Ground beef—for those who haven't had Plainville ground turkey.	
Turkey Salad 2.00			**Turkey Barbecue Style** 2.25	
Chopped turkey and celery with mayonaise.			Slices of turkey smothered in barbecue sauce on an onion roll.	
Five Pack 2.50			**Grilled Cheese** 1.75	
Bacon, cheese, tomato, asparagus and turkey on toast with our special sauce.			With bacon, ham or turkey 2.75	

Turkey Specialties

Hot Turkey Sandwich 3.50	**Plainville Club Sandwich** 3.75
Freshly roasted Plainville turkey, hand-carved to your order, served open-faced with mashed potatoes and gravy.	Generous double decker of bacon, lettuce and tomatoes to compliment your choice of turkey breast or smoked turkey breast.
Turkey In A Basket 3.75	**Turkey a la King** 3.25
Golden fried strips of turkey served with french fries and our own special sauce.	Chunky turkey a la king served with toast points over noodles or mashed potatoes.

Something Extra

Soup 95	
Turkey noodle or soup of the day.	
Small Garden Salad 95	
Lettuce, tomato, cucumber with choice of dressing.	
French Fries 95	
Mashed Potatoes with Gravy . . .95	
Turkey Dressing and Gravy . . . 1.25	
Home Made Salads 75	
Cabbage, Macaroni or Potato	

Salads

Julienne 3.50	
Turkey breast meat, turkey ham, cheese and egg on a bed of crisp lettuce with your choice of dressing.	
Garden 1.75	
Generous salad of fresh garden vegetables with dressing of your choice.	
Turkey Salad Plate 3.50	
Our chef's special turkey salad, fresh fruit and tomatoes on a bed of lettuce.	
Plainville Dieter 3.50	
Slices of fresh roasted turkey breast and cottage cheese on lettuce with fresh fruit.	

Beverages

Fruit Juice 75	
Lemonade or Iced Tea 65	
Soft Drinks 50	
Milk or Hot Chocolate 50	
Coffee, Tea 50	
Milk Shake 1.25	
Cranberry Cooler 1.25	
Tasty blend of cranberry juice and raspberry sherbet.	

Dinners

Plainville (All You Can Eat) Turkey Dinner 6.95
Same as Plainville turkey dinner and your choice of beverage and dessert, plus seconds of anything you would like (no doggie bags for this one).

Plainville Turkey Dinner 5.50		**Teriyaki Turkey** 6.25	
Fresh roasted Plainville turkey, hand carved to your order, served with dressing, mashed potatoes and gravy.		Breast meat sauteed in teriyaki sauce with peppers, onions, and mushrooms. Served over a bed of rice pilaf with gravy.	
Turkey Marsala 6.50		**Italian-Style Turkey** 5.50	
Breast meat lightly battered, breaded and sauteed in butter and Marsala wine. Served with fresh mushrooms and rice pilaf or potato.		Breaded and deep fried breast of turkey with cheese, smothered in Italian sauce and served with spaghetti.	
Turkey Cutlet 6.25		**Fresh Haddock** 4.95	
Breast meat sauteed with butter and fresh mushrooms. Served with rice pilaf or potato.		Fresh haddock lightly breaded and served with french fries and cabbage salad.	
Center Cut Pork Chops 6.95		**Turkey Pot Pie** 4.95	
Two center-cut grilled pork chops, served with apple sauce and your choice of potato.		Individual casserole of chunks of turkey and vegetables in gravy covered with a flaky pie crust.	
Turkey Ham Steak 4.95		**Fish of the Day**	
Unbelievable! Our natural hickory smoked turkey ham is served with pineapple and choice of potato.			

All of the Above Dinners are Served with Soup, Garden Salad and Breads

For Openers

Turkey Fingers 1.95	**Turkey Cocktail** 1.75
Golden fried strips of turkey breast, served with a mild mustard sauce.	Chunks of turkey breast served with tangy cocktail sauce.

For Smaller Appetites

Turkey Dinner 3.95	
Turkey, dressing, mashed potatoes and gravy.	
Pork Chop Dinner 4.50	
One grilled center-cut pork chop, served with apple sauce and choice of potato.	
Fresh Haddock 3.95	
Fresh haddock lightly breaded and served with french fries and cabbage salad.	
Turkey Pot Pie 3.95	
Individual casserole of chunks of turkey & vegetables in gravy covered with a flaky pie crust.	

Desserts
(Be sure to save room!!)

Pie 1.25	
Varies with the season, ask your waitress. Don't pass by our fresh apple pie made at the farm.	
A la Mode 1.75	
Sundaes 1.50	
Vanilla Ice Cream 1.00	
Raspberry Sherbet 1.00	

A restaurant menu from the 1980s. Meat items, other than turkey, were added from time to time but we found the customers came to the restaurant to enjoy roast turkey, which was chosen by more than 90% of our customers.

Reflections

Businesses, like buildings, need a strong foundation. My grandfather and my parents believed in hard work, honesty and fairness. I was fortunate that the stork (not the turkey, in this case) dropped me in a home with a business that espoused these values. I think some of it might have rubbed off on me and then was passed down to Mark. But, businesses also need employees (team members, in our case), whose brains, sweat and dedication make it all happen. We had hundreds of team members for whom I have the greatest respect. It is impossible for me to remember each one so I mention only the ones who were with the farm in recent years and for longer periods of time. My heartfelt thanks go out to each one.

Next to the team members, who always came first, were the millions of customers who purchased our products, some of them over several generations. A business is nothing without customers. We always tried to provide them with a quality product, not products to compete with the competition, based on price. I am forever thankful for these loyal customers that enabled Plainville Turkey Farm to be my livelihood.

My son Mark Bitz is an awesome leader and I was most fortunate to have him return to the farm when he did. Unbelievable things were accomplished during his tenure at Plainville Turkey Farm. The things he accomplished will be reverberating through society for generations and benefitting millions of consumers. He set the standards that the meat and poultry industry are gradually moving toward including producing healthy meat without using antibiotics, a common industry practice that diminishes the effectiveness of drugs when they are used to treat humans. Through improved feeding formulations for the turkeys, he was able to reduce the amount of saturated fat and cholesterol in the meat by 70%, producing a healthier product. He proved that turkeys could be grown profitably and with superior results using animal friendly practices.

Although Mark is extremely gifted and provided the leadership, it couldn't have been done without the help of an awesome group of people that put it all together.

The management team that worked with Mark, helping to accomplish the amazing, cutting-edge innovations, while rapidly growing Plainville Turkey Farm, Inc. was truly exceptional! They consisted of Nelson Bratt, Chip Hyde, Josh Allen, Bella Stahl, Barb Quijano, Tim Gaul, Roxanne Parmele and Sherri Woods. Each of them provided the day-to-day leadership to bring out the best in each team member and put Plainville far ahead of its competition. Two other long-term outstanding team members that must be singled out are Bill Rogers, who was an incredible sales representative and Janice Kline who provided exceptional quality control.

Although I have mentioned some of the truly outstanding achievements of Plainville Turkey Farm, it is worthwhile to summarize them because of their significance in putting Plainville in the lead and as actions that are gradually raising standards for the entire meat and poultry industry. Some of these innovations are beginning to move through the industry but it will take years for others to work their way through the systems.

- Pioneered the growing of turkeys without antibiotics.

- Pioneered the growing of turkeys without animal protein.

- First All Natural Special Occasion Line of products.

- First All Natural Deli Line of products.

- Winner of the national American Culinary Best Taste Award.

- First to receive the American Humane Association Free Farmed Certification.

- Winner of the American Culinary Institute Fresh Turkey Best of Show and Taste Awards.

- Trade Marked - Animal Friendly, Veggie Grown, Heart Lite, Nature's Way, Earth Wise.

- Grew turkeys using wind energy.

- Plainville became the largest supplier of turkey to some of the nation's most upscale retailers, proving recognition of the quality of Plainville Turkey.

I have had the opportunity to observe the development of the turkey industry from time of the hen setting on her nest to hatch her baby turkeys, on thousands of farms throughout the country, to the highly scientific and mechanized turkey industry of today. It has been a remarkable transformation and I am fortunate to have been a part of it and to see Plainville's leadership in many of the tremendous changes that have occurred.

Plainville Turkey Farm has been a huge part of my life from the time I was able to walk. Even today, as I sit in my home surrounded by empty turkey growing buildings and a large unused turkey processing plant I have wonderful memories of my 70 years of effort in the business. Although my work toward its success was minimal this past decade and the first two decades of my life, my heart has always been with it.

Unquestionably the turkey business took the majority of my time but fortunately I recognized there was much more to life than turkeys. My family, my community and agriculture were all important, and much of my time was joyfully spent in these activities. Each of these provides ongoing opportunity and pleasure. Even though my turkey days have ended, the joys of living continue.